The Corridors of Time · II ·

HUNTERS & ARTISTS

By HAROLD PEAKE and
HERBERT JOHN FLEURE

NEW HAVEN · YALE UNIVERSITY PRESS
LONDON · HUMPHREY MILFORD
OXFORD UNIVERSITY PRESS
1927

Printed in England at the OXFORD UNIVERSITY PRESS
By John Johnson Printer to the University

PREFACE

THE cave paintings, sculptures, and rock drawings of our hunter forefathers in south-west Europe have attracted so much of the attention both of scholars and of the public that the period when they lived and learned to express themselves so remarkably has become for many the great pre-historic age. It is not our purpose to describe again their artistic efforts in detail, but rather to think of their life and to try to estimate its great importance for human progress, remembering Professor Elliot Smith's dictum that the period of the artist-hunters is the beginning of the Neanthropic Age, the age of modern man, and thus stands in contrast to all that went before, i. e. to the Palaeanthropic Age. Did we but know more, we could doubtless see the modern races of man spreading and differentiating as they spread, learning to look before and after, dreaming of powers beyond the reach of the senses, and finding outlets for the springs of mind in many new directions. It is true that this early age of art ended in a collapse in Western Europe, but we begin to see its links with later time and have great faith that fresh discoveries will make those links ever more clear, perhaps in N. Africa, perhaps in S.W. Asia, probably in both. Negative conclusions are peculiarly at the mercy of new discoveries, but it seems at present that in the day of the hunter-artists the great discovery of methods of food production had not yet been made. This book of our series thus discusses the flowering of ancient culture prior to the rise of food production ; our two next between them will deal with the greater flowering of ancient civilization based on food production, and its decay. Four such culminations and declines can be distinguished in the story of man: the culture of the hunter-artists, the cultures of early Mesopotamia and Egypt (Dynasties I–VI), the cultures of Crete, Babylonia and the Egyptian Empire, and finally the cultures of the Classical World and the Eastern Sages. We are too near the later movements to generalize about them.

Many thanks are due to the authors, editors, and publishers of the following works and journals for permission to reproduce figures : *The Worst Journey in the World* by A. Cherry-Garrard (Constable & Co., Ltd.) for fig. 1 ; *Ancient Hunters* by W. J. Sollas (Macmillan & Co., Ltd.) for figs. 2–4, 20 and 40 ; *The Journal of the Royal Anthropological Institute*, vol. liv, for figs. 7 and 8 ; *Men of the Old Stone Age* by H. F. Osborn (Charles Scribner's Sons) for figs. 18 and 19 ; *Fossil Man in Spain* by H. Obermaier (Yale University Press) for figs. 22, 23, 27, 34, 43, 44, 48–50, 52–6, 59, and 66–9 ; *Human Origins*, 2 vols., by G. G. MacCurdy (Appleton & Co., New York) for figs. 24–6, 28–33, 36–9, 41, 42, 45–7, 57 and 64a ; *Antiquity of Man* by A. Keith (Williams and Norgate, Ltd.) for figs. 35 and 72 ; *Textbook of European Archaeology*, vol. i, by R. A. S. Macalister (Cambridge University Press) for figs. 60, 61 and 63 ; *Proceedings of the Prehistoric Society of East Anglia*, vol. iii, for fig. 62 ; *Report on the Excavations at Grime's Graves, Weeting, Norfolk* (Prehistoric Society of East Anglia) for fig. 64c ; *A Guide to the Antiquities of the Stone Age in the Department of British and Mediaeval Antiquities*, 2/e, (British Museum) for fig. 64b ; *Die Diluviale vorzeit Deutschlands* by A. Schliz (E. Schweizerbart, Stuttgart) for fig. 70; and *Proceedings of the Spelaeological Society*, vol. ii, for fig. 73.

H. J. E. P.
H. J. F.

May 1927.

CONTENTS

1. The Retreat of the Ice 1
2. Changes in the Coast-line 12
3. Tundra, Steppe, and Forest . . . 28
4. Late Palaeolithic Industries . . . 39
5. Early Types of Modern Man . . . 59
6. The Life and Thought of the Times . . 77
7. Palaeolithic Survivals 95
8. Later Palaeolithic Invaders of Europe . . 121
9. Chronological Summary . . . 135
   INDEX 151

LIST OF ILLUSTRATIONS

1. The edge of an ice-sheet. (From a photograph by F. Debenham) . 3
2. The features left at the end of a vanished glacier (after Penck and Brückner) 5
3. Map of the Baltic region, showing the retreat of the ice-sheet (after de Geer) 7
4. Banded clay, Finland (after Sederholme) 9
5. Chart showing the correlation of the late glacial stages . . 11
6. Map showing the ancient shore-line around the British Isles . 15
7. Teeth from Ghar Dalam 16
8. Diagram of the deposits in Ghar Dalam 17
9. Map of the Western Mediterranean during the Würm glaciation . 18
10. Map of Europe during the Würm glaciation . . . 19
11. Map showing the greatest extent of the Yoldia Sea . . 20
12. Map of Ancylus Lake 21
13. Map of Littorina Sea 24
14. Chart of the late glacial and post-glacial phases . . . 25
15. Map of Britain after the Ice Age 26
16. Map of Russia, showing tundra, pine, and oak forest belts . 29
17. Map of the regions of loess and related deposits in Europe . 31
18. The animals of the steppe (after H. Fairfield Osborn) . . 33

List of Illustrations

19. Outline engraving of cave-bear. From the cavern of Combarelles (after the Abbé Breuil) 35
20. Section through the deposits of the rock shelter at Solutré (after the Abbé Breuil) 36
21. Chart showing successive types of vegetation in Europe . . 37
22. Lower Capsian industry (after the Abbé Breuil) . . . 41
23. Early Aurignacian points of Châtelperron type (after the Abbé Breuil) 42
24. Audi points 43
25. Châtelperron points 44
26. Core-scrapers from the Middle Aurignacian industry . . 45
27. Late Aurignacian industry (after Breuil and Bouyssonie) . . 47
28. Proto-Solutrean industry 49
29. Lower Solutrean industry 51
30. Upper Solutrean industry 52
31. Lower Magdalenian industry 53
32. Middle Magdalenian harpoons 54
33. Upper Magdalenian harpoons 55
34. Perforated staves of reindeer horn (after the Abbé Breuil) . 57
35. Profiles of Upper Palaeolithic and Neanderthal man (after Keith) . 61
36. The Grimaldi skeletons (after Verneau) 63
37. The Grimaldi skull. (Photograph by the Abbé Villeneuve) . 64
38. The Old Man of Cro-Magnon (after Lartet and Christy) . . 65
39. The Combe Capelle skull (after Hauser) 69
40. Conventional sculpture of the horse's head (after Piette) . . 78
41. Magdalenian dart-thrower of reindeer horn, representing a mammoth (after de Mortillet) 79
42. Female statuette from the cave of Barma Grande. Aurignacian period (after Reinach) 80
43. Anthropomorphic design (after Piette and Breuil) . . . 81
44. Two bison, modelled in clay, from the cave of Tuc d'Audoubert (after the Count de Bégouen) 83
45. Drawing in red of an elephant in the cave of Castillo, near Santander. First phase of the Aurignacian period (after Alcaldi de Rio, Breuil, and Sierra) 84
46. Engraving of a bison and horse, from Les Combarelles (after the Abbé Breuil) 85
47. Painting of an ox in the cave of Font-de-Gaume (after Capitan, Breuil, and Peyrony) 86
48. Hands, silhouetted against a colour, from the cave of Castillo (after Breuil) 87
49. The Stag Hunt, from the 'Cueva del Mas d'en Josep' . . 89
50. War Dance of Archers, from 'Cueva del Civil', Castellón . . 90
51. Chart of the industries and art of the Upper Palaeolithic Periods . 91
52. Female figures from the principal shelter at Alpera, Albacete, painted in dark red 93

vi   *List of Illustrations*

53. Typical geometric flints (after the Abbé Breuil) . . . 97
54. Azilian harpoons 99
55. Spanish petroglyphs, representing human figures more or less conventionalized, compared with similar designs from the painted pebbles of Mas d'Azil 101
56. Geometric flints from Mugem (after the Abbé Breuil) . . 103
57. Tent-shaped designs (after Capitan, Breuil, and Peyrony) . . 105
58. Chart of the Mesolithic or Epipalaeolithic Period . . . 107
59. The Maglemose industry (after P. Reinecke) . . . 109
60. Objects from the Danish shell-heaps (A. P. Madsen, Sophus Müller and others, *Affaldsdynger fra Stenaldere i Danmark*, Copenhagen, 1900) 111
61. Pottery from the shell-heaps (after Madsen) . . . 112
62. Flint axes from Thatcham 113
63. Nøstvet axes (from Brøgger, *Strandliniens Beliggenhed*) . . 115
64. Picks from Campigny, Cissbury, and Grimes Graves . . 117
65. Spear-heads from Chwalibogowice, Nörre-Lyngby, and Bann . 118
66. Stone implements of Asturian type 119
67. Skulls from the cave of Ofnet, Bavaria (after F. Birkner) . . 123
68. Altar of skulls in New Caledonia (after F. Sarasin) . . 124
69. Group of skulls at Ofnet (after R. R. Schmidt) . . . 125
70. *Norma verticalis* views of 'double-curved' skulls from Ofnet . 127
71. Profile of a prognathous skull from Mugem . . . 128
72. Side and front view of the Galley Hill skull . . . 129
73. Side and front view of skull from Aveline's Hole . . . 130
74. Map of Europe during the second maximum of the Würm glaciation 137
75. Profiles of Grimaldi, Cro-Magnon, and Combe Capelle skulls . 139
76. Map showing the distribution of the Proto-Solutrean industry . 141
77. Europe in 2nd Würm maximum 143
78. Map showing the distribution of the Tardenoisian industry in Europe 147
79. Map showing the distribution of the Nörre-Lyngby culture . 149

I
The Retreat of the Ice

IN the first part of this series we have seen that in the last great geological period, the Pleistocene, many parts of the world were subject intermittently to extremely frigid conditions, which are collectively known as ' the Great Ice Age ', and that contemporary with this are our first certain evidences of the existence of human life.

We noted that most observers believe that the Ice Age was fourfold, that glaciers flowing from the snow-fields reached much farther down the valleys than at present, while large ice-sheets, similar to that now covering Greenland, enveloped much of both land and sea north of 52° N. latitude.

Our last chapter closed with an account of the fourth, the Würm glaciation, which, though the areas covered by snow and ice were not quite so extensive as during some earlier ice ages, was sufficiently severe to make most of Europe uninhabitable, or at the best to render conditions between the northern ice-sheet and the Alpine snow-fields as severe as the coldest areas in Siberia to-day. Up to this time such human beings as we know of from their skeletal remains were very unlike any men that we find living in the world to-day.

After the retreat of the Würm ice, or indeed while it was in the process of retreating, modern man, *Homo sapiens*, first makes his appearance in Europe, and the following pages will be devoted to describing his form, his works, his civilization, and the environment in which they were evolved.

When the Würm glaciation was at its height the snow-fields in Central Europe reached down nearly 2,000 ft. below their present level, while the glaciers extended down still farther. From Scandinavia a great ice-sheet covered the whole of the Baltic region and Finland and came southwards far enough to cover a strip of North Germany. Snow-fields and ice-sheets existed in the British Isles.

If a snow-field does not melt, the snow cannot run off as water, but gradually slides down the slopes into the valleys, where it becomes compressed into ice. This ice moves slowly down the valleys till it reaches a level at which the air is warm enough to melt it. Such streams of ice are known as glaciers, and may be seen in the Alps and other high mountains to-day.

As the glacier proceeds slowly down the valley, its edges scrape the mountain-sides, grinding the rock to mud and causing blocks to fall upon its surface ; the glaciers have thus on either edge a line of mud or broken rock, known as a lateral moraine. The base of the glacier, too, grinds the surface beneath it into mud, which it pushes along ; this mud, with the fragments of rock carried on its surface, becomes deposited in a crescent-shaped heap across the valley where the glacier melts. This is known as a terminal moraine. The mud and stones beneath the glacier form a ground moraine.

If for many centuries a glacier melts at the same spot, the terminal moraine grows large ; if, however, owing to a gradual change to warmer conditions the melting-place of the glacier is slowly retreating up its valley, the terminal moraines are slight, though they increase in size when the melting-place becomes again constant. Such large terminal moraines have been noted at many places in the Alpine valleys and elsewhere, and similar masses of mud and rock, but extending over many miles, can be seen in Scandinavia and North Germany, showing where the melting-margin of the northern ice-sheet was constant for many centuries. By mapping such moraines it has

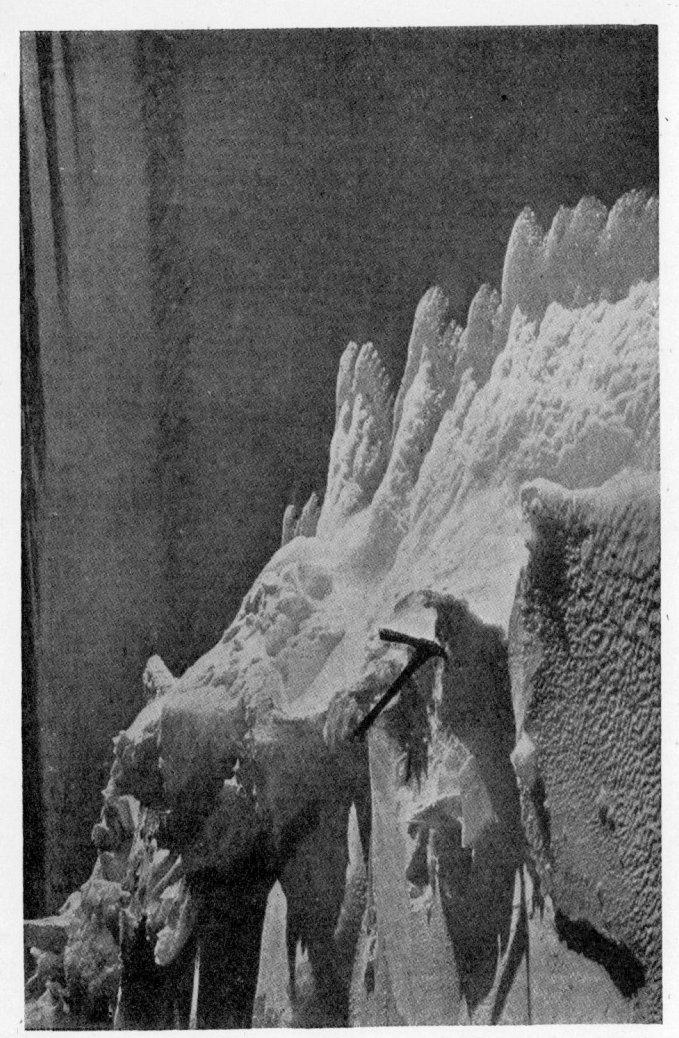

FIG. 1. The edge of an ice-sheet. (From a photograph by F. Debenham.)

been possible to trace the gradual stages in the retreat of glaciers and ice-sheets.

After the maximum of the Würm glaciation came a shrinkage called the Laufen retreat, but only of relatively short duration; then a fresh onset of cold gradually carried snow, glaciers, and ice-sheets almost as far as before. This is known as the second maximum of the Würm glaciation. At length, at a time which has been variously estimated as 17,000 or 15,500 years ago, or at 15,000 or 13,500 B.C., the extreme conditions began finally to pass away, and the snow and ice to retreat.

The first period of retreat was very slow and by no means uniform, for, although for a time there was a slight amelioration of the climate, there was often for an interval a slight return of the ice. This period of gradual but intermittent retreat of the ice has been called the Achen oscillation, and seems to have lasted for about 5,000 years or more. Then for many centuries the ice and the glaciers advanced once more, though not nearly so far as they had done during the maxima of the Würm. This readvance of the ice is known as the Bühl advance.

Since Penck and Brückner first put forward their views, as summarized here, they have, as a result of further investigations, somewhat modified them with regard to the first part of this glacial retreat. They think now that the second maximum of the Würm glaciation was by no means as intense as they first believed, but that the snow and glaciers then advanced but little farther than they did in the Bühl phase. They now believe, too, that the second maximum was not a single episode, but a succession of advances of a similar degree of intensity. Again, during the Achen oscillation they believe that, although on the whole the ice and snow retreated, yet on more than one occasion they advanced almost as far as they did in the

Bühl phase. They think also that the Bühl advance was not a single episode, but that during this period, which must have lasted for some centuries, the glaciers advanced on three occasions and remained for some time in this forward position on each advance. It is to this period that they attribute the remains of three terminal moraines which are to be seen in the neighbourhood of many Swiss lakes. The name Bühl thus shares the fate of many another name in geology and becomes a mere label without special reference to the original Bühl moraine.

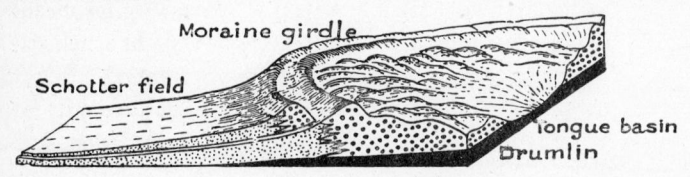

FIG. 2. The features left at the end of a vanished glacier (after Penck and Brückner).

After the Bühl stage the climate again improved, and continued to do so steadily, but with two marked pauses. These two pauses in the retreat are known as the Gschnitz stage and the Daun stage. These names, Achen, Bühl, Gschnitz, and Daun, have been taken from Alpine valleys, where evidence of these stages are to be seen, and their initial letters represent the first four letters of the Greek alphabet, a, β, γ, δ.

So far we have been dealing with evidence collected mainly in the Alpine region of Central Europe by Professors Penck and Brückner; we must now turn to Scandinavia and the Baltic region, where the successive stages of the ice retreat have been worked out with greater precision by Baron de Geer, the Swedish geologist, and his disciples.

There is a line, running parallel to the southern shore of

the Baltic Sea, and distant from it between twenty-five and fifty miles; along this line there is a heaped-up mass of clay and boulders, considered to be a terminal moraine. The line crosses Jutland from west to east just north of latitude 54°, then bears southwards about twenty-five miles inland from the Baltic coast, and later turns eastwards, diverging still farther from the coast, until it reaches the borders of West Prussia. Thence it passes south in a great curve, crossing the Vistula at Warsaw, and passing northwards to the entrance of the Bay of Riga. Behind this line is a bed of boulder clay, left by the retreating ice-sheet of the north.

Apparently in its retreat northwards the edge of this ice-sheet halted again for a while along the southern coast of Norway, thus forming another heaped-up mass of clay and boulders called the Ra moraine; this runs parallel to the coast to a point near the extreme south of Sweden. Here this moraine takes a sharp turn westwards for some miles, then passing round the island of Zealand and across the south of Funen, follows the Baltic coast southward and eastward to near Rostock, after which it continues its way about twenty-five miles from the coast to the borders of West Prussia.

The first of these lines has been called the Daniglacial moraine, and the second the Gothiglacial, while the space between the two is known as the area of the Daniglacial retreat, and that between the second line and a third to be described is termed the area of the Gothiglacial retreat.

After forming the Gothiglacial moraine, the edge of the ice-sheet retreated once more, coming to a halt along a third line, also showing much morainic accumulation, that passes close to the second along the south-east coast of Norway. This moraine, crossing the southern ends of Lakes Wener and Wetter, reaches the Swedish coast south of Stockholm; after that it

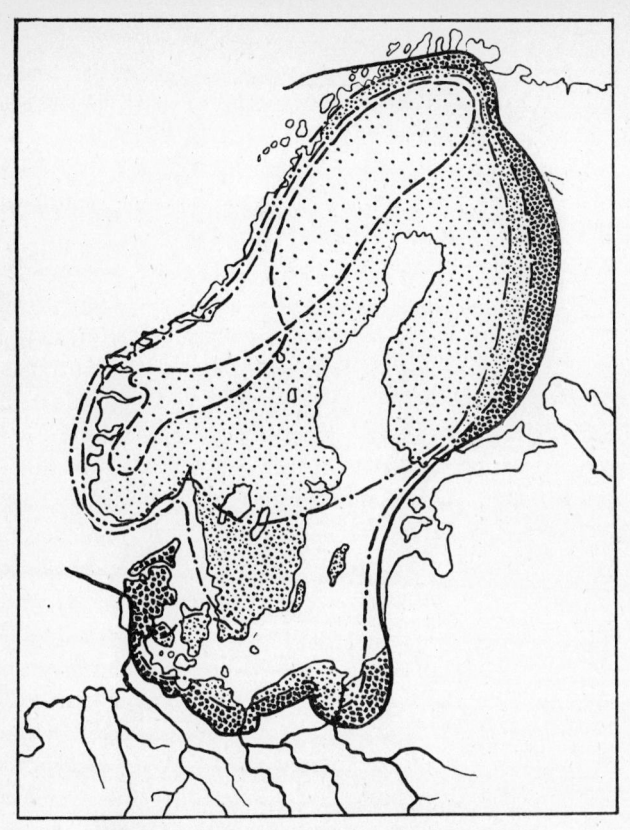

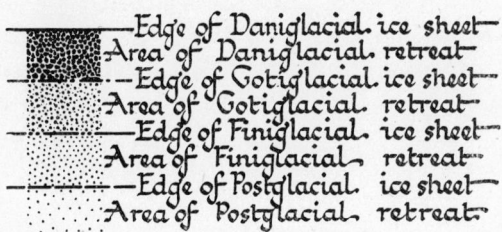

▬▬▬ Edge of Daniglacial ice sheet
▰ Area of Daniglacial retreat
─·─·─ Edge of Gotiglacial ice sheet
▨ Area of Gotiglacial retreat
─── Edge of Finiglacial ice sheet
▒ Area of Finiglacial retreat
······· Edge of Postglacial ice sheet
░ Area of Postglacial retreat

FIG. 3. Map of the Baltic region, showing the retreat of the ice-sheet (after de Geer).[1]

[1] Enquist thinks that the region of the Norde Fjord, the Lofotens and Romsdal were ice-free at the beginning of the Finiglacial retreat.

crosses the Baltic to the south-western corner of Finland. This line is called the Fennoscandian moraine, and the area between it and the highland backbone of Scandinavia is called the area of the Finiglacial retreat. By the time that the edge of the ice-sheet had retreated to these highlands the Ice Age was at an end, for no glaciers were left in the lowlands, and all that remained was the snow-fields on the heights.

Now de Geer's view is that the Daniglacial moraines show the extent of the last great glaciation, while the Gothiglacial and Fennoscandian moraines show two great pauses or re-advances of the ice-sheet. Again, at Lake Ragunda, just at the limit of the Finiglacial retreat, he has found evidence of another pause in the retreat of the ice, which is known as the Ragunda pause, only just before the ice disappeared.

The deposits laid by the ice over these areas of retreat are clays laid down in very thin layers, each layer representing, it is believed, the mud laid down each summer as the ice-sheet retreated. De Geer and his pupils have counted these layers at many places, and have related the different samples by studying their relative thicknesses. By this means they have estimated the period which elapsed during the Gothiglacial and Finiglacial retreats, and the results of these were published in 1910. Since then they have been carrying out similar measurements in North America.

The latest calculation published is given by Sollas. Lidén has estimated the end of the glacial retreat, when the ice-sheet finally disappeared, as 8,500 years ago, or about 6500 B.C. In November 1923 de Geer wrote, ' the guess may be ventured that the commencement of the Gothiglacial sub-epoch may be found to lie some fifteen to sixteen thousand years beyond the present day ', that is to say, about 13,500 B.C. If we assume the rate of retreat across Sweden to be fairly uniform,

FIG. 4. Banded clay, Finland (after Sederholme).

we may consider the beginning of the Finiglacial retreat to have taken place about 8500 B.C., and if, following Sollas, we allow a period of 5,000 years between the beginnings of the Daniglacial and the Gothiglacial retreats, we must place the former at 18,500 B.C. When de Geer's final calculations are made known, it is possible that some adjustments will have to be made in these figures; it is unlikely, however, that the changes will be of serious extent.

We must now turn to Scotland, and for this country we have the pioneer work of James Geikie. In his Munro Lectures in 1913 he recognized six glacial epochs as occurring in Scotland. These he termed, beginning at the first, the Scanian, the Saxonian, the Polonian, the Mecklenburgian, the Lower Turbarian, and the Upper Turbarian.

In England, as we have seen in the first part, Boswell recognizes a cold period, then three glacial periods, the last of which is represented by the intensely chalky boulder clay; later than this is another cold period represented by the subarctic deposits at Ponder's End in the Lea valley.

There is at present no absolute agreement as to the correlation of these different stages. Brøgger, the Norwegian archaeologist, has suggested that the Ra moraine in South Norway should be equated with the Bühl advance in the Alps, and de Geer has considered the Ra moraine as the western continuation of the line crossing the Swedish lakes, which he considers the most advanced line before the Finiglacial retreat; on the other hand, some recent writers equate the Ra moraine with the Gothiglacial. But the equation between the Bühl advance in the Alps and moraines of the Swedish lakes, the Fennoscandian moraine, has been accepted by many authorities, and if so, the Daniglacial and Gothiglacial lines must mark the limits of the greatest advances of the two maxima of the

DATE	SCANDINAVIA After de Geer & Anter	SCOTLAND After James Geikie	THE ALPS After Penck & Brückner	
2000 B.C.	Historic time			2000 B.C.
2000	Post Glacial		Daun	2000
4000	time	Upper Turbarian	Gschnitz	4000
6000	RAGUNDA PAUSE	Upper Forest	Bühl iii	6000
8000	FENNOSCANDIAN MORAINES	Lower Turbarian	Bühl ii	8000
10000	Gothiglacial retreat	Lower Forest	Bühl i Achen oscillation	10000
12000	GOTHIGLACIAL MORAINE	Mecklenburgian	WÜRM II	12000
14000				14000
16000	Daniglacial		Laufen	16000
18000	retreat		retreat	18000
20000				20000
22000	DANIGLACIAL MORAINE	? Mecklenburgian	WÜRM I	22000
24000				24000

Fig. 5. Chart showing the correlation of the late glacial stages.

Note. The chart reads, in order of time, from the bottom upwards.

Würm, while the Ragunda pause, which was of considerable duration, must be the equivalent of the third Bühl advance in the Alps.

The Scottish equations are more difficult still, but it has been suggested that the first four enumerated by James Geikie, the Scanian, Saxonian, Polonian, and Mecklenburgian, should be equated with the four great Alpine glaciations, the Günz, Mindel, Riss, and Würm, while the two lesser ones, the Lower Turbarian and the Upper Turbarian, represent respectively the Bühl and the Gschnitz. These equations can better be understood by reference to the table on p. 11.

BOOKS

SOLLAS, W. J. *Ancient Hunters,* 3rd Edn. (1924).
BROOKS, C. E. P. *Evolution of Climate,* 2nd Edn. (1925).
GEIKIE, James. *The Great Ice Age* (1887 and 1894).
   ,,   ,,   *Prehistoric Europe* (1881).
   ,,   ,,   *The Antiquity of Man in Europe* (1913).

2

Changes in the Coast-line

THERE is also evidence that during the Ice Ages similar, though smaller, movements have taken place. Around many parts of the coast of the European region, from Scotland to North Africa, we find raised beaches, which indicate that the sea was once higher than at present; these raised beaches can be shown to be of Pleistocene date. River terraces and shore-lines, probably corresponding to these, have been noted in Mesopotamia. It has been claimed by the French geologists,

Depéret and Lamothe, that four such raised beaches, which can be traced from the Mediterranean to Scotland, can be correlated to the four terraces in the valleys of many rivers. We may be certain, therefore, that four times during the Pleistocene, the sea rose above its present level.

Again, it has been pointed out that rather more than a 100 fathoms or 600 ft. below the present sea-level there are evidences of an old shore-line, in some places represented by what appear to have been cliffs. It may be that there is more than one such sunken shore-line, but evidence of this kind is difficult to obtain, and is rapidly concealed by fresh maritime deposits.

Osborn, writing as a zoologist, believes that the land was elevated during interglacial times, for it was during these times that land animals could best pass from one land mass to another; he would hence conclude that during the periods of glaciation the land was depressed.

On the other hand, as we have seen in a previous chapter, it has been suggested that it was during the cold periods that the land rose, and that this rise was one of the causes, perhaps the main cause, of the glaciations. This is the view that we are inclined to accept; it is further supported by the evidence produced by Depéret, that the shells found in the raised beaches in the Mediterranean—at any rate in the last three of them—belong to species of molluscs which dwell now in warmer seas. Thus the depression of the land, which these beaches denote, took place when the climate was somewhat warmer than at present.

The question is not, however, quite as simple as has been stated above. Even Depéret has admitted that the raised beaches, which he believes to be contemporary, are not all at the same level to-day. In addition to a general rise and fall of the coast-line, there have been certain differential movements. For instance, towards the close of the Ice Age we find evidence that the Baltic coast of Denmark was moving in an opposite direction to that on the North Sea coast, as though the land were on a see-saw with the pivot running down the centre of Jutland. Another such see-saw appears to have occurred in the British Isles, with its support running across Lancashire and Yorkshire, so that England was raised while Scotland was depressed, and vice versa.

With so many uncertainties and complications, it is not possible to restore with precision the outline of the European region during the various phases of the Pleistocene, but some attempt will be made in the following pages to indicate the probable position of the coast-line during the Würm glaciation and the retreat of the ice.

Let us first take the Mediterranean basin. During the Würm maximum we should expect the coast-line to be below the present mean sea-level. A relatively small lowering of the coast-line would cause the emergence of a land bridge between Sicily and Tunis, and might also have closed the Straits of Gibraltar, for they have been much deepened since those days.

By the shore of a little bay on the south-east side of Malta lies the village of San Giorgio a Mare, and into this bay opens a ravine known as Wied-x-Dalam. In the side of this ravine, and some feet above its bottom, opens a cave known as Ghar Dalam or the Cave of Darkness. The bottom of this cave is filled with many feet of red soil, lying in different layers, which must have been deposited at different times; the excavations which have been carried out there on various occasions between 1865 and 1918 throw some light on our problem.

The cave seems to have been hollowed out by the sea at some time when the coast-line was higher than at present,

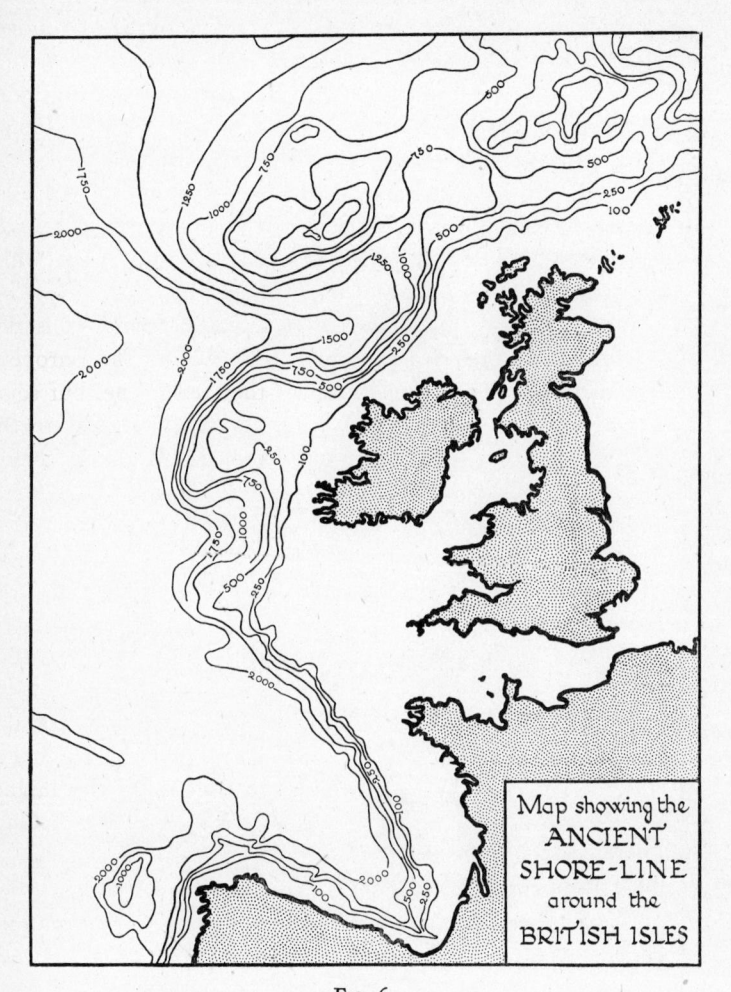

Fig. 6.

which would have been in some interglacial period. The bottom three layers contain large quantities of fragments of bones of elephant and hippopotamus, which, from their rolled condition, must have been washed in by the sea. But in the highest of these layers, the third or, according to one account, the fourth, there are numbers of small round pebbles which

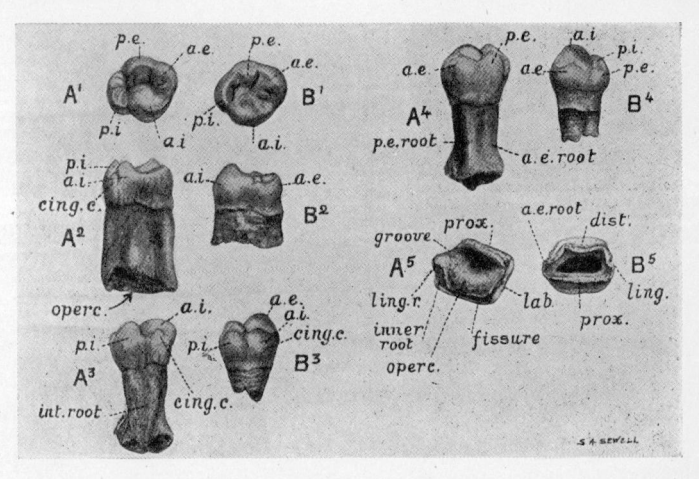

FIG. 7. Teeth from Ghar Dalam.

suggest a shore-line. While the third layer was being deposited the land had risen almost to its present level. In this layer, but apparently near the top of it, was found the fragment of a human milk molar of large size.

In the layer above this, the second layer, there were no signs of water-worn remains; the floor of the cave was evidently well above the sea-level, and there is no clear evidence that the water has since returned. In this layer, among many remains of the bones and antlers of the stag, were found a number of human teeth of varying type. One of these, however, was a large milk molar, with fused roots, very closely resembling that found in the layer beneath. In the top layer were found

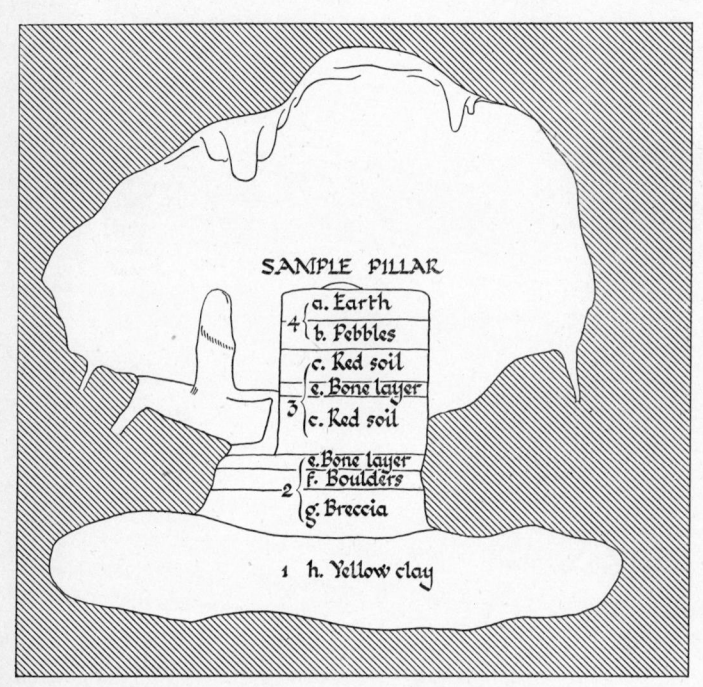

FIG. 8. Diagram of the deposits in Ghar Dalam.

the remains of modern animals and fragments of pottery dating from neolithic and later times.

The evidence as it stands is somewhat perplexing, but the various items fall well into place if we imagine that the fragment of the molar, found in the third layer, had either slipped into a crack at a later time, or had been carried down by some burrowing animal. Its unrolled condition, in which it differs from other fragments from the third layer, which all show signs of having been worn by the action of water, makes this explanation the more plausible.

Now these two molars are almost identical in form; the complete one from layer two shows the roots fused into a single

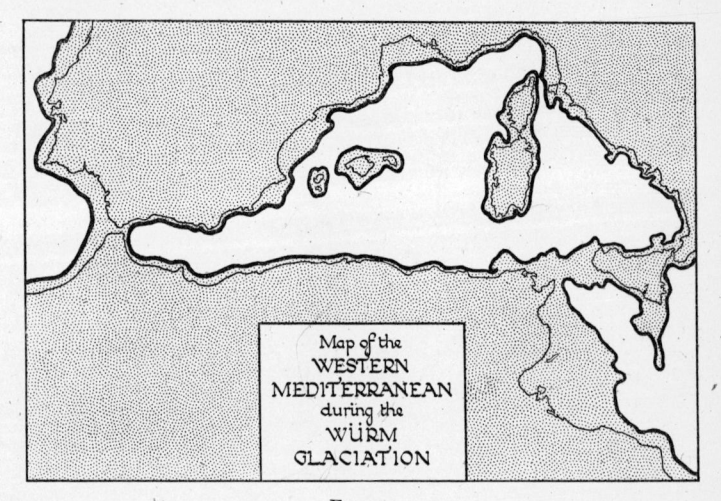

Map of the
WESTERN
MEDITERRANEAN
during the
WÜRM
GLACIATION

FIG. 9.

one. This condition of the teeth, known as taurodont, has been found among some representatives of Neanderthal man; the Maltese specimens in this and other respects closely resemble those from the cave of Krapina and the teeth discovered by Dr. Marett in Jersey. We find, therefore, that the evidence from the cave shows us that at one time the sea rose many feet around the island of Malta, and swept into the cave fragments of bones of elephants and hippopotami. Gradually the sea retreated until small rolled pebbles were swept in at high tide.

Then the cave rose well above the sea-level, and naturally the deposits were formed more slowly. In due course it was occupied by a type of man whose teeth show that he may well have been related to Neanderthal man, though one must

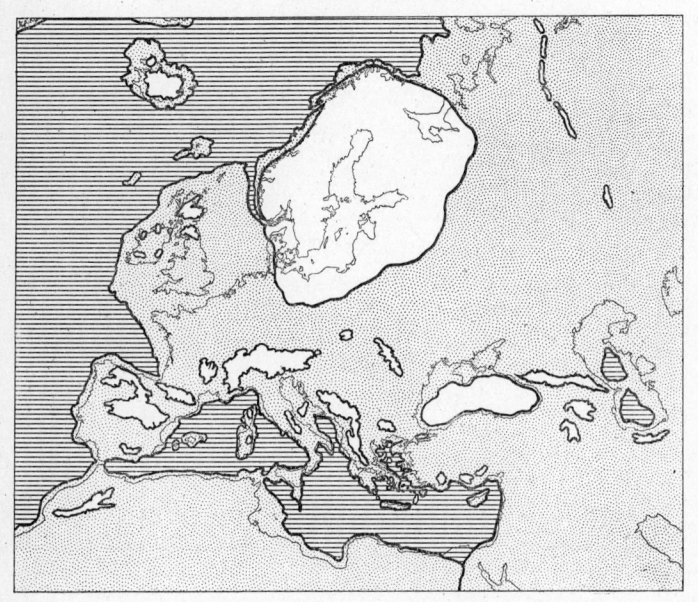

FIG. 10. Map of Europe during the Würm glaciation.

not argue too definitely from a mere tooth. Later, during the deposition of the top layer, it was occupied by neolithic and later inhabitants.

This sketch of physical history, however, raises an important question, namely, how did man of a possibly Neanderthal type reach the island. We can hardly believe that he had so far developed in civilization that he could use a boat, a canoe, or even a raft. It is no more likely that he could swim eighty miles. We are therefore forced to conclude that he came by dry land, and that during the deposition of the second layer

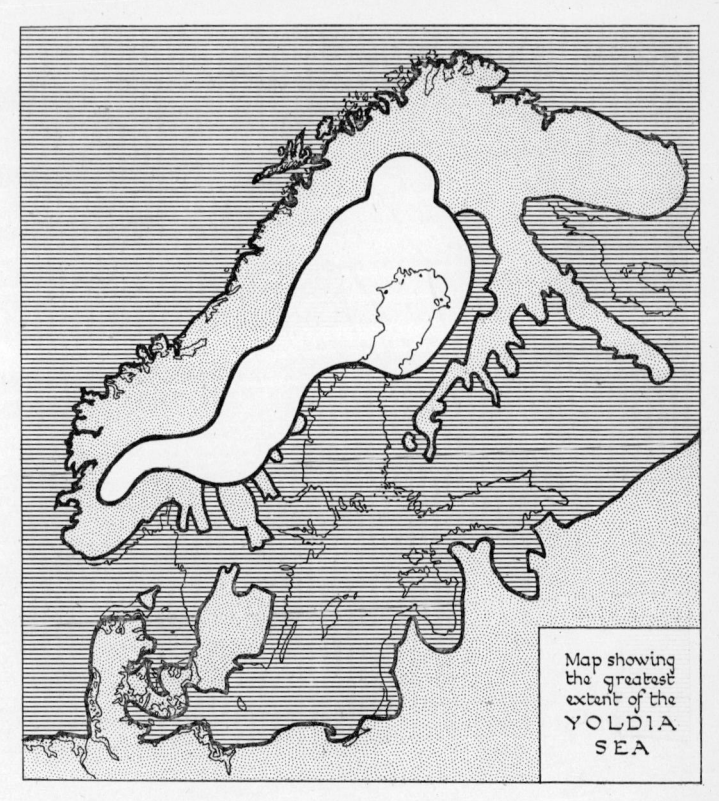

Map showing the greatest extent of the YOLDIA SEA

Fig. 11.

the land rose sufficiently to connect Malta with Sicily and Italy on the one hand, and with North Africa on the other. The elevation of the island by 600 ft., or perhaps even less, would join Malta to Sicily, and a somewhat greater elevation would have united the west end of the larger island with the coast of Tunis.

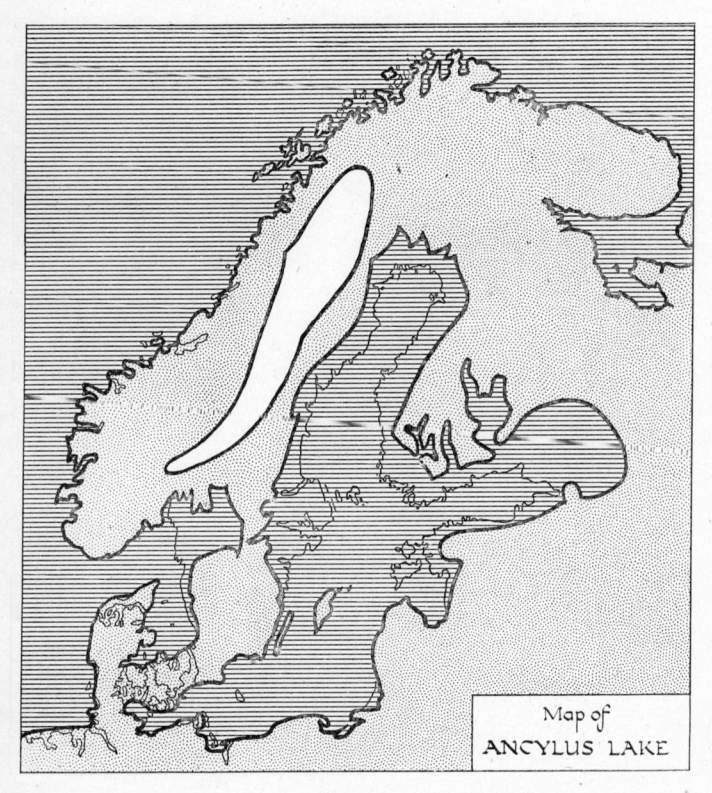

FIG. 12.

Map of ANCYLUS LAKE

The question of the Straits of Gibraltar is more difficult, for these are relatively deep, and some experts think that a channel has been open since early Pleistocene times. But on two occasions, the second of which may with fair certainty be equated with the Bühl advance of the ice, we have evidence of the appearance in Spain of a culture from North Africa, and in these early days an advance of culture must mean an invasion of the people to whom it belongs.

We must picture, then, the Mediterranean during the Würm glaciation as consisting of two inland seas, with their coast-lines rather more than 600 ft. below the present sea-level. In the western of these was a large promontory, stretching from Italy near Leghorn, and including Corsica and Sardinia; there were several large islands, including a combined Majorca and Minorca. The eastern sea had an outline very different from that of the present eastern Mediterranean. Most of the Adriatic was dry land, the Aegean was smaller, and the majority of its islands connected with the shores on either side or forming long promontories, but special local movements may have occurred here. There may also have been dependent inland seas or lakes in this eastern region, but existing charts do not allow us to decide whether they did or did not drain into the eastern sea. On the other hand, as the alluvium of the delta had not yet been formed, it seems likely that a more or less torrential Nile, running through an area of fairly heavy winter rainfall, emptied itself into a deep bay.

On the whole we may assume with no little probability that during the Achen oscillation the sea gained somewhat on the land, perhaps even burst through the Straits of Gibraltar, but that with the Bühl advance the land rose again, though not to so great a height, but sufficient to enable men to cross from Africa to Spain, even if not quite dryshod. Then the land sank, perhaps for a time below the present coast-line.

In the Baltic region this problem has been studied in greater detail, though it is impossible to begin as early as the Würm glaciation, for the area now occupied by that sea was then under the northern ice-cap. It is believed, however, that the Arctic Ocean then occupied not only what is now the White Sea, but extended thence south-westwards over part of Russia and as far south as Königsberg. As the edge of the ice-sheet retreated northward across the Baltic in the Gothiglacial retreat —which we believe to have been contemporary with the Achen oscillation—the land sank over east Scandinavia, though Denmark and Norway seem to have remained much as at present. This sinking of the land allowed the northern ocean to stretch from the White Sea to the Cattegat, and to submerge South Finland, the Baltic States, and a large part of south Sweden. As the ice continued its retreat the sea extended farther northwards. From a mollusc found very commonly in the clays laid down in the bed of this sea it is called the Yoldia Sea; it seems to have increased to its full size during the latter part of the Gothiglacial retreat, and to have shrunk during the Fennoscandian cooling contemporary with the Bühl advance. The Baltic floor rose, leaving the greater part of the sea an inland lake, called from the prevailing mollusc found in the mud laid down in its bed, the 'Ancylus Lake'; it seems to have lasted until after the Ragunda pause, which we equate with the third Bühl advance in the Alps.

After this the southern part of Scandinavia sank, the Ancylus Lake became connected again with the North Sea. The waters were fairly warm, for it would appear that the period immediately following the Gschnitz stage was slightly more genial than at present, at any rate in the northern parts of Europe; in these warmer waters flourished the periwinkle (*Littorina littorea*), from which the Baltic, as it was at this time, is called the Littorina Sea. This slight extension of the Baltic lasted, it is thought, for several thousand years, during the latter part of which period the land around it rose slowly to its present level, which seems to have been attained about 200 B.C.

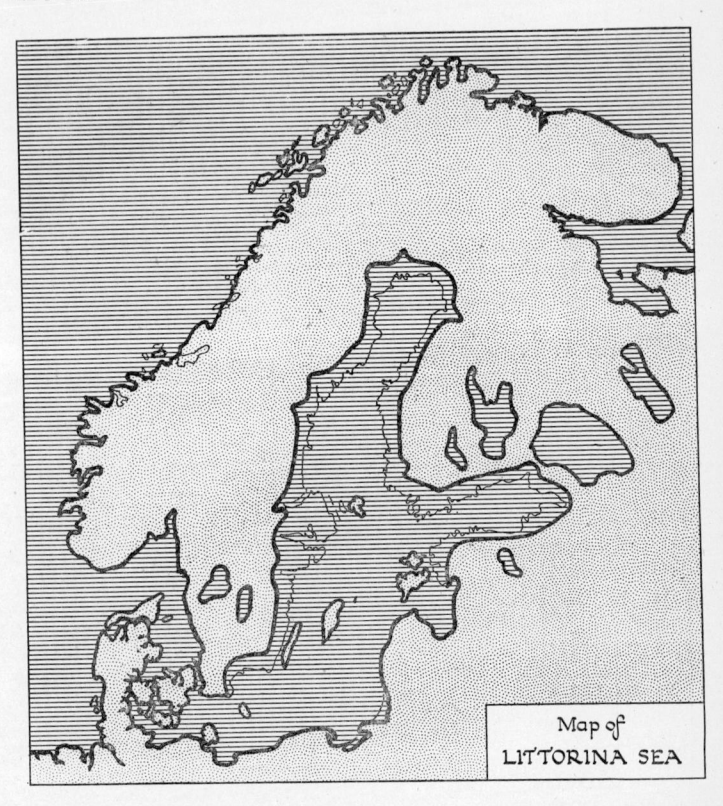

FIG. 13.

Map of LITTORINA SEA

In Scotland, too, we have evidences of changes of level. At the beginning of the period in which the Yoldia Sea covered the Baltic, Scotland was depressed about 130 ft., and we have beaches at this level almost all round the country. Then the

DATE	SCANDINAVIA: Retreat of Ice, After de Geer & Lidén	SCANDINAVIA: Changes of level, After E. Anters	SCANDINAVIA: Stages in the Baltic modified from H. Munthe and others	SCOTLAND: After J. Geikie	THE ALPS: After Penck & Brückner	DATE
B.C.						B.C.
1000						1000
			LITTORINA SEA		DAUN	
2000						2000
3000	Post-Glacial Time	Submergence Tapes	Salinity twice that at present	25^{ft} beach		3000
4000				Upper Turbarian		4000
		ELEVATION	ANCYLUS LAKE		GSCHNITZ	
5000		Submergence	Fresh water Inland Sea	Upper Forest		5000
6000	RAGUNDA	ELEVATION		50^{ft} beach	BÜHL III	6000
7000	Fini-glacial retreat	Submergence	YOLDIA SEA			7000
8000						8000
	FENNO-SCANDIAN MORAINES	ELEVATION	South Baltic Ice Lakes & Inland Seas	Lower Turbarian	BÜHL II	
9000		Submergence			BÜHL I	9000
		ELEVATION				
10000						10000
11000			Scania free from ice	Lower Forest		11000
12000	Gothiglacial retreat	Submergence $141^m = 463^{ft}$		100^{ft} beach	Achen oscillation	12000
13000						13000
14000	GOTHIGLACIAL MORAINES	ELEVATION		Mecklenburgian	WÜRM II	14000

Fig. 14. Chart of the late glacial and post-glacial phases.

Note. The chart reads, in order of time, from the bottom upwards.

land rose, but sank again towards the close of this period, and remained for a time stationary at 50 ft. below its present level,

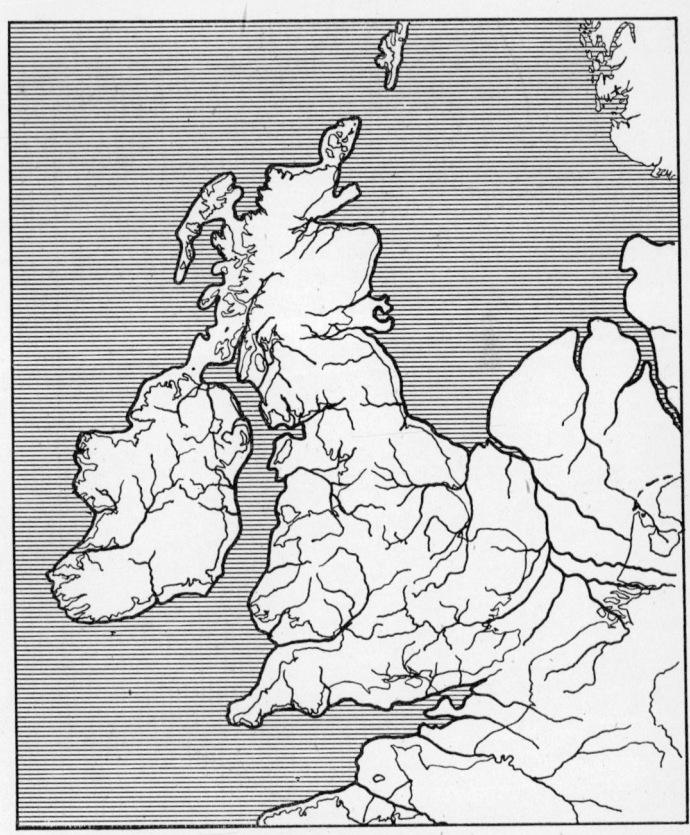

Fig. 15. Map of Britain after the Ice Age.

causing the 50 ft. beach which survives along much of its coast. During the Ancylus period the land rose again, but towards its close sank 25 ft. below its present level, leaving the 25 ft. beach ; finally, it came to an approximate rest at its present level.

No clear evidence of similar changes has yet been noticed in England, for the raised beaches in Sussex, described by Dr. Palmer and Lieutenant-Colonel Cooke, belong to earlier times ; nor have we any similar evidence from the coasts of France or the Iberian peninsula. It is, however, probable that somewhat similar changes must have taken place.

The late Dr. Clement Reid has studied the coast-lines of a period which he believed to have been a part of the Neolithic Age ; this was probably the elevation which occurred during the Gschnitz stage. The sea-level was then some 90 ft. lower than at present, and the south part of the North Sea, nearly as far north, at any rate, as the Dogger Bank, was land. This condition is believed to have coincided with the earlier part of the period of the Littorina Sea, but may well have begun earlier still, perhaps before the close of the Ancylus period.

BOOKS

SOLLAS, W. J. *Ancient Hunters* (1924).
KEITH, A. *The Antiquity of Man* (1925).
REID, Clement. *Submerged Forests* (1913).

Tundra, Steppe, and Forest

IN many of the forests of Denmark there are small but deep depressions, known as *skov-möse*, filled up with layers of peat. Around these depressions, which once were lakes, trees have grown, and some of these on attaining maturity have fallen into the water and sunk to the bottom. Thus the peat has preserved successive layers of tree trunks, which enable us to form some idea of the different types of forest which grew round the lakes. At the bottom of these depressions is usually a layer of peat containing no conspicuous vegetable remains, indicating that during its formation no forest was growing near; then come layers of pine trunks, higher up layers of oaks and white birches, while near the top are layers of the common birch, which, with the beech and spruce, are the commonest trees to-day.

Careful investigation has shown that during the time of the Yoldia Sea the prevailing plant was the *Dryas* or mountain Avens, indicating an Alpine or tundra flora. Then, during the period of the Ancylus Lake, forests of pine grew up, with wych elm and hazel in places. The climate, though less severe, was sub-arctic, like that obtaining in North Russia to-day, but, before the disappearance of the lake, a still milder climate followed, and oak trees began to appear. The oak forests flourished best during the period of the Littorina Sea, but as this period drew to a close they were replaced by the beech forests which are found there to-day.

The Danish evidence is very valuable as showing the types of woodland which have succeeded one another in the southern Baltic during the time of the Finiglacial retreat, or since the

FIG. 16. Map of Russia, showing tundra, pine, and oak forest belts.

Bühl advance. Earlier than this, during the Gothiglacial retreat, which we have equated with the Achen oscillation, the evidence is scanty, and we can only infer an arctic climate with a tundra vegetation. For the rest of Europe we have no such clear evidence, and we are forced to draw conclusions from the types of animals whose bones have been left in cave deposits. On the Russian plain to-day we find successive belts of tundra, pine forest, and oak forest as we pass southwards from the Arctic Ocean. One thing, however, we must remember: at no time has the vegetation been the same all over Europe. There must always have been belts, depending on the parallels of latitude, or more accurately speaking the isothermal lines, varied, however, by the altitude. There would also have been, as there are to-day, local differences, due to prevailing winds, the amount of rainfall, the nature of the soil, and other conditions.

As the Würm glaciation passed away, increasing areas in the European plain lost their covering of ice. Nevertheless for a considerable time the ice-sheets were still large. Moreover, the innumerable heaps of mud and boulders hindered the free run off of the abundant water. In some parts of the northern plain the drainage is still imperfect, and we find vast extents of marsh and lakes; of this type are the historic 'Masurian Lakes' in East Prussia, while the meres of North Shropshire owe their origin to similar causes. For a long time, then, after the maximum of the Würm there must have been many lakes and swamps on the plain, while the winters were still too severe and snowy to allow the growth of trees.

Masses of cold air at high pressure doubtless lay over the plains of Europe during the winter time, so that storms occurred around their margins, and these raised dust from the mud left by the retreating ice. The gradual re-establishment of a drainage system enabled the water in the lakes, which we have already mentioned, to find its way to the sea; thus the extent of dry land was increased and the dust storms were commoner. These great dust storms usually came from the

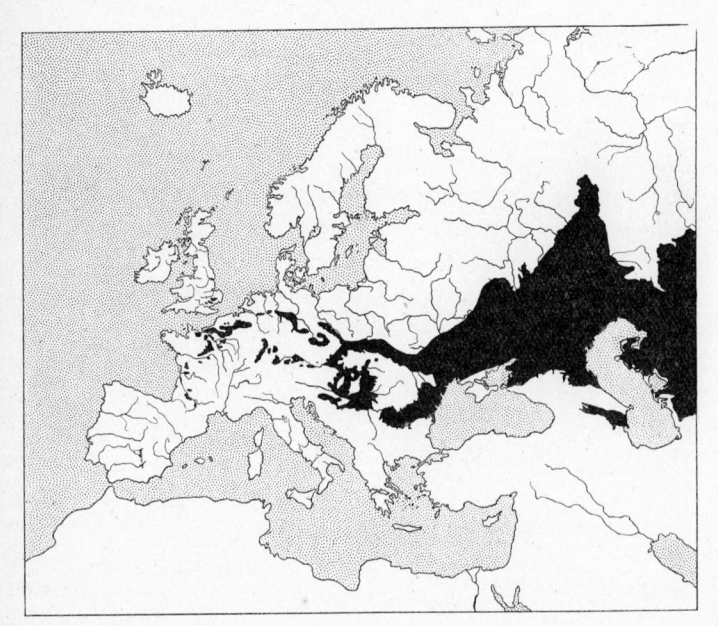

FIG. 17. Map of the regions of loess and related deposits in Europe.

edge of the ice-sheet, and carried great quantities of fine-grained soil, and deposited this in several basins, such as **Bohemia** and **Hungary**; much of this fine dust accumulated against the northern slopes of the Central European highland, from the Harz mountains eastward to south-west Russia; much also was blown across the Russian plain.

This fine-grained soil, which is called 'loess', has played

an important part in the rise of civilization. It is more suitable for the growth of grass than of trees, and, as the grass dies down and decays each winter, this soil has become very fertile. The fact that it has been free from dense forest, even when the climate was favourable to such growth, has always kept it open country. For these reasons, and especially the last, it has been a zone which men have chosen for movement and for settlement at many periods.

Water was, in all probability, abundant in those early times at certain seasons of the year, especially when the ice and snow melted in the spring; we know that land freed from snow by sunshine grows grass very rapidly. Thus we may feel sure that there was good grass over increasingly large areas in Europe, and this afforded grazing for herds of animals, among which we may picture diminishing numbers of reindeer, the woolly mammoth and woolly rhinoceros, and another grass-eating rhinoceros from Siberia, usually known as the Elasmothere; there were also animals related to the sheep, the horse, and the wild ass of the steppes. Where water was abundant and the grass long and rich, there would have been some bush or scrub; here would roam the bison and the urus, the forerunner of the ox. The musk-ox, however, lived nearer to the snow.

It is important to remember that the European plain had been flanked on the one side by the northern ice-sheet and on the other by the Alpine snow-fields with their glaciers. As a result, its preglacial and interglacial plants had been exterminated rather than driven south. The plants which were now spreading seem to have come, for the most part, from Asia, and comparatively few southern forms appeared for some time. In this respect there is a sharp contrast between Europe and North America, for in the latter continent, where

FIG. 18. The animals of the steppe (after H. Fairfield Osborn). The saiga antelope, the (A) steppe hamster, the (B) great jerboa, and the kiang, or Asiatic wild ass.

the mountains form ridges directed north and south, the plants retreated southwards as the ice advanced, returning northwards when it retreated. The flora which now covered Europe was mainly composed of different kinds of grasses, and man fed mainly on the flesh of grass-eating animals; what sources of vegetable food he may have had is still a mystery, but in the Atlantic region it seems likely that the blackberry was beginning to spread.

In the early part of the period which we are now considering the lemming, an Arctic rodent, still lived as far south as Portugal; as the climate improved these retired northwards, even faster than the reindeer. About this time a giant deer (*Megaceros*) first came into this country. The chief beasts of prey inhabited the caves, namely the cave-lion, cave-leopard, cave-hyena, and cave-bear, but the wolf and the wild cat had already arrived. It is interesting that some of these larger forms had survived from interglacial times. It is unwise to lay down a definite rule, but we know that large beasts are often specially able to keep warm in cold climates and to accumulate reserves against a foodless season.

It is usually stated that during the early part of the Achen oscillation the surface of the European plain was still largely tundra, a name which conveys too easily to many minds the notion of a scant covering of mosses and lichens with dwarf birch and Arctic willow. Even if Stefansson is too enthusiastic, he has at least shown us that Arctic regions of tundra have a relatively rich summer flora of sedges, grasses, dandelions, bluebells, poppies, anemones, primroses, and other plants, and he states that for every ton of mosses and lichens there are at least ten tons of these richer and quicker growing plants. This description helps us to picture the ancient European tundra on which some varieties of dock or sorrel also appeared before long. It is quite possible that dandelion and sorrel and some little bulbous plants helped to feed mankind, and that their collection provided work for the women who could not run with the hunting pack. The occurrence of the wild cat, brown bear, red deer, and roe deer suggests that forests were growing here and there. We should also note that widespread sheets of water suggest fish food, a suggestion which is strengthened when we remember that the otter was then spreading in Europe.

FIG. 19. Outline engraving of cave-bear. From the cavern of Combarelles (after Breuil).

Any advance of the ice, even a small one, would be heralded by increased cold, with hard, dry winters, dust storms, and a further accumulation of loess. That this was happening late in the Achen period is very clear from many lines of evidence. We shall see that at this time a civilization, known as Solutrean, spread westward into Europe, especially on the loess lands, preceded by a great spread of the horse. Vast quantities of horse bones have been found in the lower layers of the famous section at Solutré in France. These horse bones are doubtless in large measure the debris of the meals of the men and women of that region, especially before the culture invasion just mentioned. The invasion reached westward to the coast of Spain, north of the Cantabrian mountains, but it is doubtful whether it extended south of the great mountain line formed by these heights and the Pyrenees. Later on the Saiga antelope, an Asiatic cold steppe animal, spread into Europe, and reached as far as Mentone. When the cold was most intense the lemming and reindeer were men's comrades in western Europe, but in the later part of this phase the steppe became richer, and the loess afforded a zone of expansion westwards for Asiatic animals.

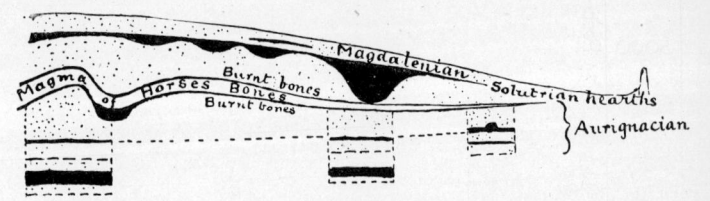

FIG. 20. Section through the deposits of the rock shelter at Solutré (after the Abbé Breuil).

The Arctic willow and dwarf birch seem to have given way to pine forests as the Bühl advance was approaching; these came in from the south-east and spread specially towards the north-west, but they do not seem to have covered very large areas in the south-west nor to have lasted a long time. Steppe conditions may well have survived on many of the patches of loess in Central Europe, but, as the steppe of the loess lands and elsewhere grew richer from the decayed grasses, the pine forest seems to have retreated uphill and northwards, and with it vanished the reindeer. The companions of the pine included the wych elm and the hazel, and the extent of this forest increased as more of Scandinavia became free from the ice sheet. Towards the end of the Ancylus Lake period in the Baltic there was an elevation of the land and a corre-

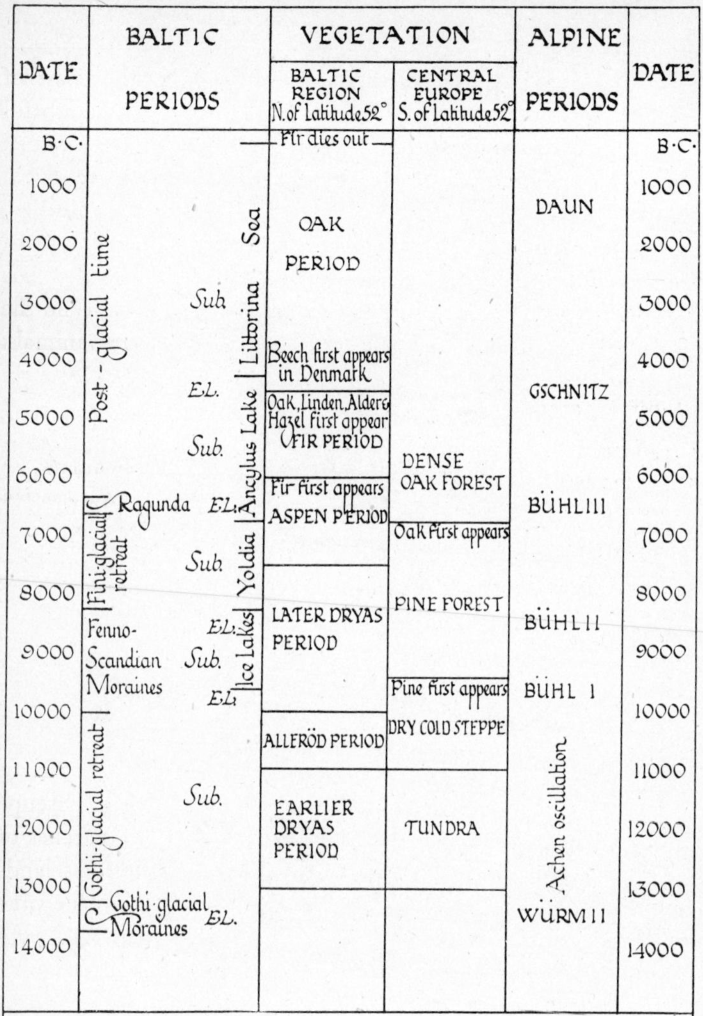

DATE	BALTIC PERIODS	VEGETATION		ALPINE PERIODS	DATE
		BALTIC REGION N. of Latitude 52°	CENTRAL EUROPE S. of Latitude 52°		
B.C.		Fir dies out			B.C.
1000	Post-glacial time / Sub / EL. / Sub. / Ragunda EL. / Finiglacial retreat / Sub. / Fenno-Scandian Moraines / EL. / Sub. / EL. / Gothi-glacial retreat / Sub. / Gothi-glacial Moraines / EL.			DAUN	1000
2000	Littorina Sea	OAK PERIOD			2000
3000					3000
4000		Beech first appears in Denmark		GSCHNITZ	4000
5000	Ancylus Lake	Oak, Linden, Alder, Hazel first appear (FIR PERIOD)			5000
6000		Fir first appears ASPEN PERIOD	DENSE OAK FOREST	BÜHL III	6000
7000			Oak first appears		7000
8000	Yoldia	LATER DRYAS PERIOD	PINE FOREST	BÜHL II	8000
9000	Ice Lakes				9000
10000		ALLERÖD PERIOD	Pine first appears DRY COLD STEPPE	BÜHL I	10000
11000				Achen oscillation	11000
12000		EARLIER DRYAS PERIOD	TUNDRA		12000
13000				WÜRM II	13000
14000					14000

Fig. 21. Chart showing successive types of vegetation in Europe.

Note. The chart reads, in order of time, from the bottom upwards.

sponding cooling of the climate, which we may equate with the Gschnitz stage in the Alps. After this came a fresh depression with a milder climate, inaugurating in the Baltic the condition known as the Littorina Sea.

The pine forest was now retreating fast. The oak now became an important part of the flora of north-west Europe, while the red deer and the roe deer became the characteristic animals. The large beasts of earlier times now disappeared, and with them, and perhaps also as a result of the improved hunting methods of the men of that time, went some of the most dangerous of the cave-dwelling beasts of prey. The giant deer vanished from the European mainland, while hares and rabbits arrived in western Europe from the south. The pine forest, however, remained in possession of the surface in many regions, of which Bavaria seems to have been one, and this is an argument against the too early dating of certain finds at Ofnet, with which we shall deal in a later chapter.

We have already seen that the last amelioration of the climate is to some extent linked with extensive land sinkings in north-west Europe. These sinkings had serious influences upon the repopulation of what became the North Atlantic island group. It is a remarkable fact that the west of the Spanish peninsula and the south-west corner of Ireland share several peculiar plants and animals, such as the winter strawberry, the London pride, the great spotted slug, and a peculiar lacustrine shellfish. This so-called 'Lusitanian' association may be supposed to have lived on the Atlantic coast-lands of the Ice Age. As the climate improved the flora spread landwards, but old coast-lands sank, so it is now found on separate peninsulas and islands. These sinkings must have been very rapid, as otherwise this flora would surely have survived more distinctly in places between Spain and Ireland.

In this connexion we may find some interesting contrasts between Jersey and Guernsey. Guernsey was certainly an island long before Jersey was separated from the Continent, for when the ten-fathom line was the shore, Jersey and Les Minquiers were still peninsulas. Guernsey lacks the snakes, toads, and moles of the larger island. Similarly, the separation of England from the Continent delayed or prevented the arrival of plants and animals. Also the absence of snakes from Ireland is an indication of still greater hindrances in the case of the farther island.

4

Late Palaeolithic Industries

BREUIL thinks that the Neanderthal men of Mousterian culture lived in western Europe from the time of the Riss on through the Würm glaciation, and there is some evidence that they were here, too, when the second maximum was past and the ice had begun its retreat. It seems possible that with the advent of the cold they retreated from the northern latitudes and from the higher lands, not only in the Alpine area, but in central France and northern Spain, and, while many crossed the Mediterranean to the shores of Africa, where numerous remains of their industry have been found, others were content to stay in caves on the northern shore. The Mousterian remains near Mentone may well be post-Würmian in date, while it is said that those found in the cave of Pocala, west of Trieste, belong undoubtedly to the time of the glacial retreat.

As the ice continued its retreat during the Achen oscillation a new industry appeared, in many ways different from those which we have met with hitherto. From the place in which it was first noted, a small rock-shelter, now quarried away, at Aurignac in the Department of Haute-Garonne, this industry is known as Aurignacian, or the industry of Aurignac.

Though it was new to Europe, a similar industry, which appears to be antecedent to it, has been noted at Gafsa, in Tunisia, the ancient Capsa. This has been termed Capsian, and the early forms, which are believed to precede Aurignacian, are known as Lower or Early Capsian. This culture, which includes as a new feature the use of long thin flakes of flint, often finely worked, especially at one end, is found distributed along the southern shore of the Mediterranean Sea, especially from Tunisia to Morocco. It has not yet been found with certainty farther south, and in the coastal area seems to occur in two cultural regions, an eastern or *Getulian*, and a western or *Ibero-Maurusian*, each of which displays characteristic differences. As far as one can judge from the distribution of early Aurignacian sites in Europe, no approach was made across the Iberian Peninsula, for no true Aurignacian sites have yet been met with except in the extreme north of Spain. On the other hand, a number of examples of this industry have been found in the peninsula of Italy and in Sicily, from which we may conclude that it was by this route that the advance into Europe was made.

In the matter of date we may conclude that the Aurignacian industry arrived in Europe early in that period known as the Achen oscillation. It is, of course, possible that the Capsian industry had passed from Tunis through Sicily to Italy during, or even before, the Würmian glaciation, though no positive evidence pointing to this has yet been published; but, even should it turn out that this had been the case, it would have been impossible for the new-comers to cross the Alpine barrier during the intensity of the glaciation, and the way was only a little easier via the Riviera.

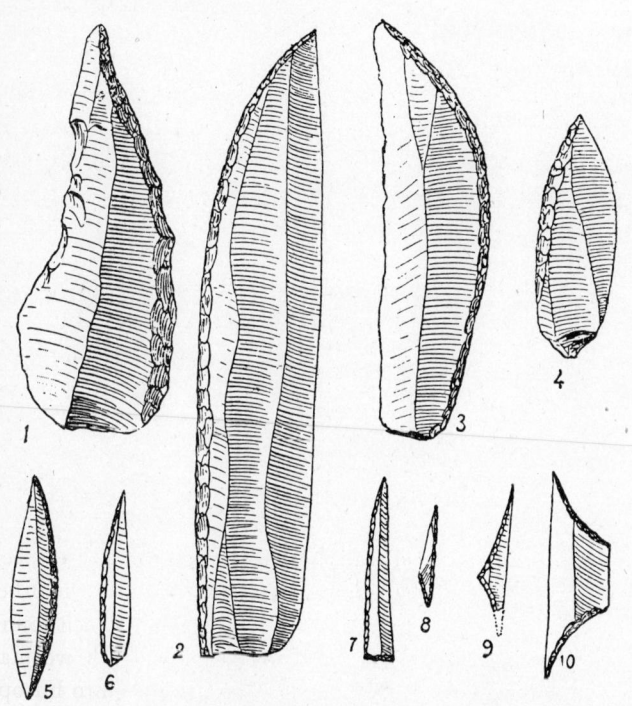

FIG. 22. Lower Capsian industry (after the Abbé Breuil).

The Aurignacian culture is usually divided into three stages, termed the Lower, Middle, and Upper. There is, perhaps, some reason for distinguishing a still earlier phase, such as has been found most typically at the rock-shelter at Audi near Les Eyzies in the Dordogne. On the other hand it is said by others that, since the characteristic Audi tool is found with considerable frequency throughout most Lower Aurignacian deposits, the remains from Audi should be considered as belonging to the earliest part of the Aurignacian period.

It will be remembered that the earliest palaeolithic implements, those of pre-Chellean, Chellean, and Acheulian types,

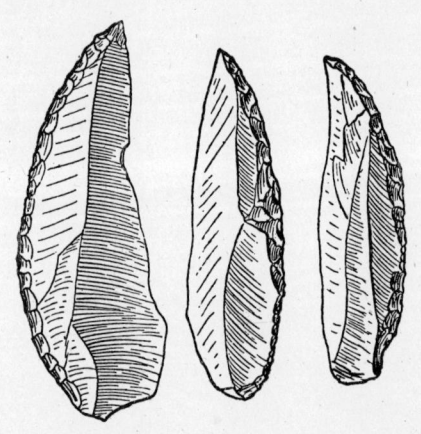

FIG. 23. Early Aurignacian points of Châtelperron type (after the Abbé Breuil).

were mostly core implements, fashioned from a block of flint by removing flakes from its surface until the desired form had been achieved. Flake implements, or those formed by working up the edges of the flakes struck from a core, only came into gradual use in Acheulian times, and even then were not common. In contrast with these the Mousterian industry was mainly a flake industry, and core implements became relatively scarcer as the period advanced. The new industry, the Aurignacian, contained much fewer core implements, while the flake implements were longer, narrower, thinner, and more delicately worked.

The Audi industry made special curved points on implements, some of which are side-scrapers (Fig. 24, 5). There

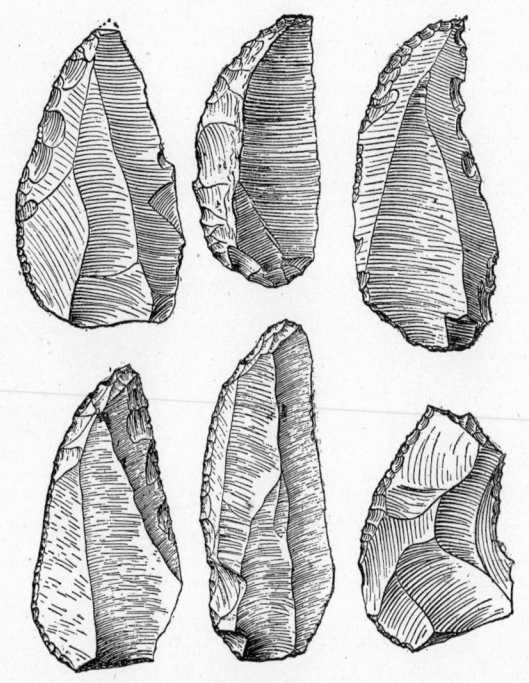

FIG. 24. Audi points.

are also *coups-de-poing* and notched tools. The curved points, known generally as Audi points, are really small knife-blades pointed at the ends; the flake is worked to a sharp edge along one side, while the other has been purposely blunted so as to be held more conveniently in the hand. These Audi points occur, though not commonly, in other deposits of Lower Aurignacian Age, and some have been found among the Lower Capsian deposits of Tunisia. The majority of the implements from the Audi shelter are definitely Aurignacian in type, but most of the side-scrapers and scrapers show some

FIG. 25. Châtelperron points.

resemblance to Mousterian forms, while some are quite indistinguishable from them. Implements of these types occur elsewhere between the Lower Aurignacian deposits and those of the Upper Mousterian, notably at the cave of Pair-non-pair (Gironde). It is generally agreed by those who have most closely studied the subject that the Aurignacian industry did not develop from the Mousterian, but from the Lower Capsian

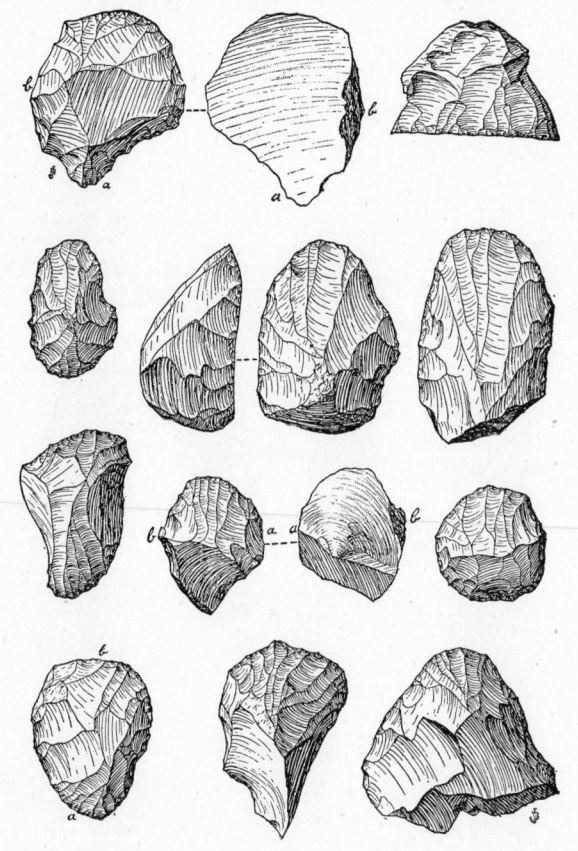

FIG. 26. Core-scrapers from the Middle Aurignacian industry.

of North Africa, but, as some of these Audi forms seem to show Mousterian influence, it is believed that the people responsible for these two industries must have come into contact, and that the Aurignacian adopted some of the finer Mousterian models. Whether this contact was made in France, in Italy, or even in North Africa, is not yet clear.

While we may distinguish the Audi deposits as belonging to a phase earlier than the Lower Aurignacian, to the latter period we must attribute the remains found at La Ferrassie (Dordogne) and Châtelperron (Allier), though these may not be quite contemporary, for the implements at La Ferrassie are thought to be somewhat earlier than those at Châtelperron. The blades from these sites are stout, with notches on the sides, sometimes single, at others opposite or alternate. Here we find keeled scrapers, of a massive form but carelessly made, and more rarely gravers trimmed obliquely. Bone implements appear for the first time, such as bone points, sometimes with a split base, known as *Points d'Aurignac*, awls, arrow-straighteners, and polishers. The distinguishing type of this period is the Châtelperron point, which is not unlike the Audi point, but smaller and finer, while the blunting of one side is effected by the removal of narrow parallel flakes.

In Middle Aurignacian times the same types continued, but the keeled scrapers, often made from cores, became more numerous and varied in form. Different kinds of gravers came into use, and the trimming of the flints reached its finest development, though towards its close a period of decadence had set in. Throughout Middle Aurignacian times bone tools became commoner, and towards their end a fresh form of tool, the La Gravette point (Fig. 27, 1–5), made its appearance; this tool seems to have developed first in Africa,

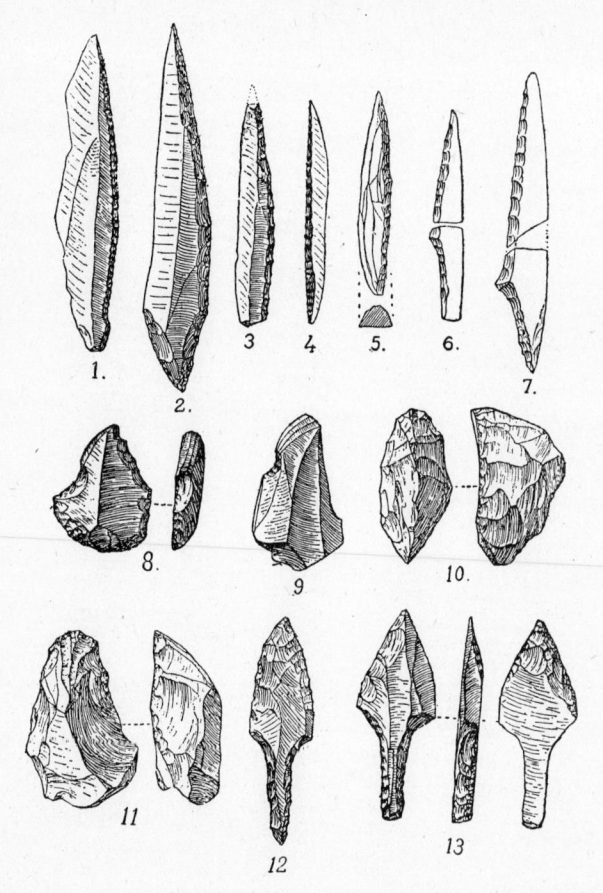

FIG. 27. Late Aurignacian industry (after Breuil and Bouyssonie).

and its appearance in Europe during the Middle Aurignacian period suggests fresh arrivals from Africa, this time across Spain.

The La Gravette point is specially characteristic of Upper Aurignacian deposits, which contain proportionately fewer flint and more bone implements. Gravers are of still more variable forms, while the points develop a side-swelling at the base, and gradually change into the single-shouldered point, sometimes, though rarely, into the double-shouldered point, which is more characteristic of the next period.

Aurignacian deposits are found over most parts of Europe, except the extreme north and the Alpine region of Central Europe. They are found in France, Belgium, the north of Spain, and the south of England, and over such parts of Germany, Poland, Bohemia, and Austria as lie at relatively low levels. They are found also in Italy and Sicily, where the Capsian affinities are more marked, and in Russia, Roumania, Bulgaria, and Syria. During Lower Aurignacian times tundra conditions prevailed over all Europe except the Mediterranean region; during Middle Aurignacian times somewhat milder and perhaps drier conditions prevailed, while in Upper Aurignacian times throughout the plain of North Europe cold steppe conditions supervened.

With this a new people and culture reached Europe, as we shall see, from the east. This new industry, which was first recognized at Solutré near Macon in the Saône valley, is called Solutrean, and is quite different from what preceded it. The characteristic implements, though perhaps made from flakes, are worked all over, and have the appearance of very fine and thin core implements, and it has been suggested that they may have developed, through many stages, from very fine flat implements of St. Acheul type. If this were so, the evolution did not take place in western Europe, nor in all probability in any part of that continent, but it may well have occurred in the steppe-lands of western Asia, such as Turkestan, the archaeology of which is as yet almost an unknown quantity.

The Solutrean industry exhibits three phases, each showing

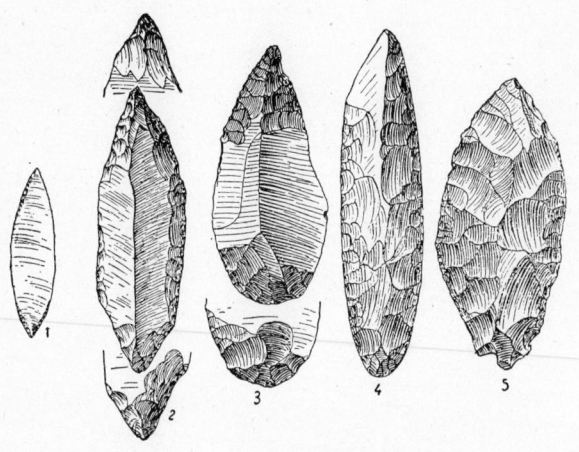

FIG. 28. Proto-Solutrean industry.

its own distinctive features, and each having its area of distribution. These are known as the Proto-Solutrean, Lower Solutrean, and Upper Solutrean. All show to a greater or less extent the new technique, which includes a high finish by the process of pressure-flaking, that is to say the removal of small thin flakes by pressing near the edge with a bone tool rather than by striking with another stone.

This pressure-flaking is already seen even in the rude Proto-Solutrean examples of the 'laurel-leaf' blades, which attain a much greater perfection later. Other implements show flakes removed by striking, as did those of the Upper Aurignacian period. The Proto-Solutrean industry is found in its most perfect condition in Hungary, which the Aurignacian industry never reached, and in Moravia, where it shows more signs of admixture with Aurignacian characters; it is found, too, in Belgium, to some extent in the British Isles and in the north of France, while it extended southwards in the west as far as the Dordogne, and down the Saône and Rhône valleys as far south as the Department of Ardeche. No type of Solutrean industry has been found in the Alpine region of Central Europe, while in its earlier phases the culture seems more characteristic of the plain than of the mountains.

In Lower Solutrean times the true laurel-leaf blade occurs in profusion, and bone implements are also found. This industry is found abundantly in Hungary, Moravia and Poland, in Bavaria, the Rhône basin and western France, and it penetrates the northern rim of Spain. Again its distribution shows that it is prevalent rather in the plains than the hill country.

In the Upper Solutrean layers the laurel-leaf blade still occurs, but the shoulder-point, which was characteristic of the Upper Aurignacian industry, reappears. This revival of Aurignacian workmanship is confined to western France south of the Loire.

The first Solutrean hunters following wild horses and cattle westwards were few, and not expert makers of weapons, though they had acquired the pressure-flaking technique. These settled among the Aurignacians, forming, perhaps, an aristocratic class. Later, more and more arrived, with a superior technique, and perhaps the skill of the Aurignacians, when they had learnt the pressure-flaking technique, improved the quality of the weapons. The new-comers kept chiefly to the

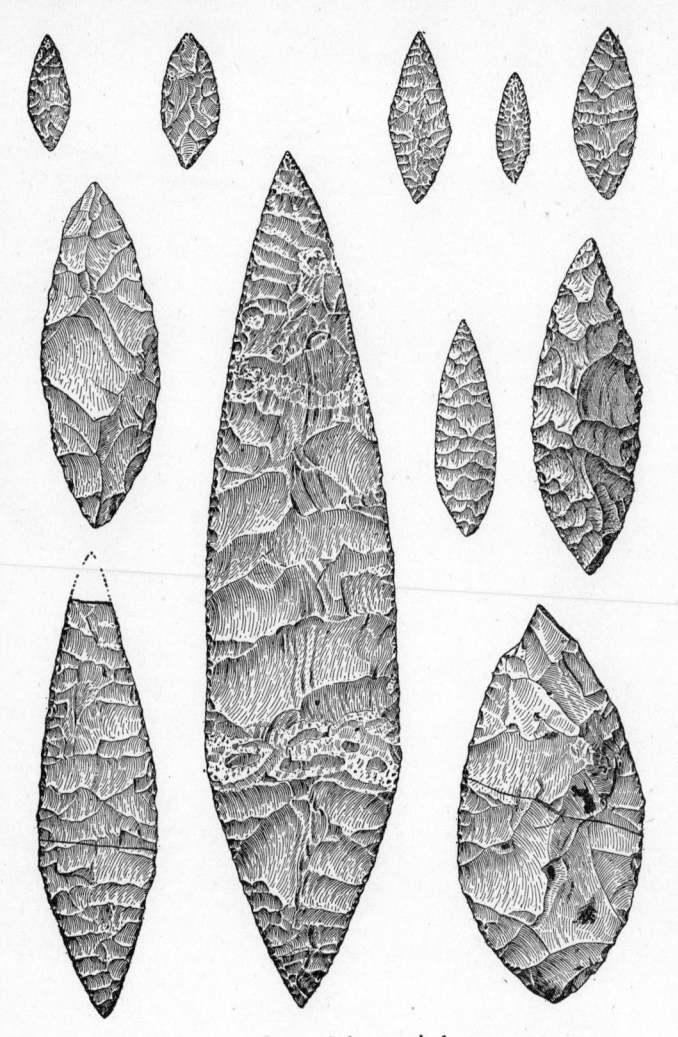

FIG. 29. Lower Solutrean industry.

plains, though at times they penetrated the mountain valleys of the Dordogne: then, as the climate grew damper, and the forests began to encroach upon the steppe, they followed their

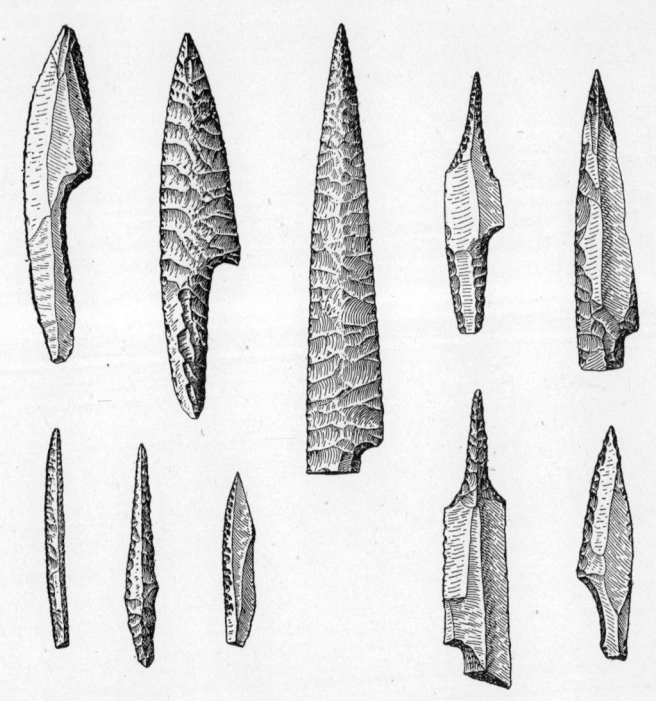

FIG. 30. Upper Solutrean industry.

prey back to the east, where the climate remained drier. Some remained for a time in south-western France, cut off, it may be, by the encroaching pine forests. These gradually merged with the Aurignacian aborigines.

The cave deposits show that the Solutrean culture was followed by another industry, which is known as Magdalenian,

Late Palaeolithic Industries

from the rock-shelter of La Madeleine in the Dordogne, which was first explored by Lartet and Christy in 1863 and 1864. This industry resembles in many respects that of Aurignac, so much so that until 1906 it was believed to be the same. It was at the International Congress of Prehistoric Archaeology, held that year at Monaco, that the Abbé Breuil

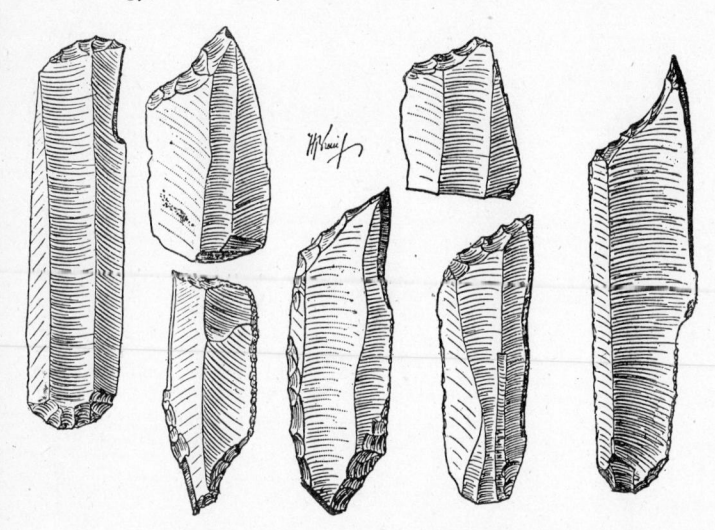

FIG. 31. Lower Magdalenian industry.

demonstrated that some stages of this industry preceded, while others followed that of Solutré, and made the suggestion that the earlier phases should be termed Aurignacian.

The Magdalenian industry is therefore but a continuation of that of Aurignac after the departure of the Solutrean hunters, and owes little, if anything, to their technique. The work is indeed much rougher, and the pressure-flaking is never found; furthermore, the Magdalenian industry consists less of flint implements than of weapons and tools of bone and horn, which reach a high quality before the close of the period.

The evidence from animal remains suggests that during the Upper Solutrean period the storm zone, which had up to now

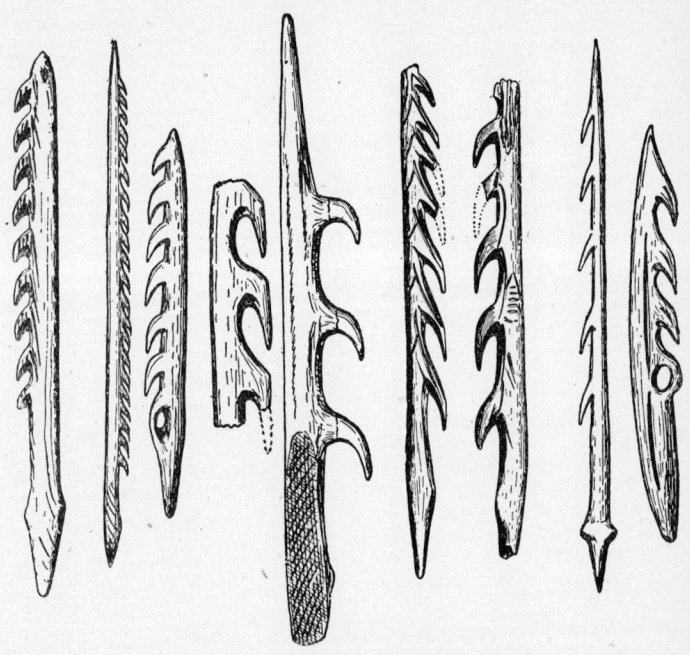

FIG. 32. Middle Magdalenian harpoons.

passed across the Mediterranean region, had moved farther north and swept along the European plain, bringing increased precipitation and a moister air. This change led the coniferous woodlands to spread into more northerly latitudes, followed in turn by forests of deciduous trees. Before the advancing forest the steppe animals, wild cattle, horses, and antelopes, retreated

Late Palaeolithic Industries

to the north and east, the reindeer held its own for a time, but gave way gradually to the red deer, and left entirely for the north as the oak forest advanced. The increased precipitation included an increase of snow and an enlargement of the snow-

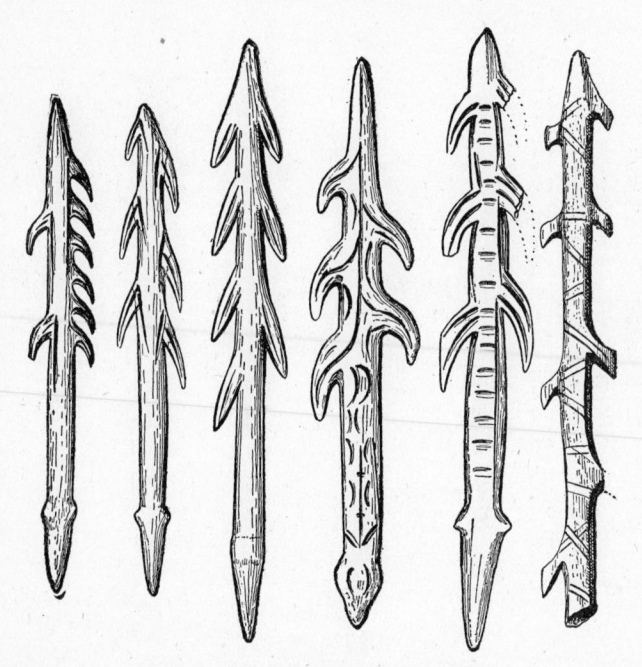

FIG. 33. Upper Magdalenian harpoons.

fields and glaciers in the Alpine region that is indicated by the Bühl advance.

The fact that stations containing remains of the Magdalenian industry have been found in Switzerland within the limits of the Würm moraines shows that these stations date from a post-Würmian time. That the bones of animals found with them are those of creatures accustomed to an Arctic climate, while those associated with the Solutrean industry are inhabitants of the steppe-lands, makes it as certain as can be that the Magdalenian industry dates from the time of the Bühl advance.

Like the Aurignacian industry, the Magdalenian has been divided into three main phases, Lower, Middle, and Upper; but the lower phase, at any rate in south-western France, has been subdivided again into four lesser phases, which may thus be tabulated :

Upper Magdalenian   6
Middle Magdalenian   5
Lower Magdalenian { 4 3 2 1

In these various stages we may trace the progressive advance of the bone industry. For instance, in the first three stages lances are found but no harpoons; the latter appear in Magdalenian 4 in a very primitive form, while Magdalenian 5 is distinguished by the presence of harpoons with a single row of barbs, and Magdalenian 6 by those with double rows. Again, in the earlier phases the reindeer is plentiful and the red deer relatively scarce ; the latter increase in number and the former grow fewer as the period advances, indicating the approach of woodland conditions.

A strange implement of this period is that which is sometimes called the perforated stave, the ceremonial stave or *bâton de commandement*. Such implements are made of the antlers of stag or reindeer, and have a hole, sometimes several, in the lower end. Their use has been variously interpreted, and they have been considered as insignia of office, toggles for

Late Palaeolithic Industries

belts, and arrow-straighteners; a more recent and plausible explanation suggests that they were used to remove kinks in raw-hide ropes. They are found, though rarely, in Aurignacian deposits, but are more characteristic of Magdalenian times, when they are of better workmanship and often decorated.

Some French archaeologists are inclined to limit the term Magdalenian as an industry, though not as a period, to the civilization found in the south-west of France and the north

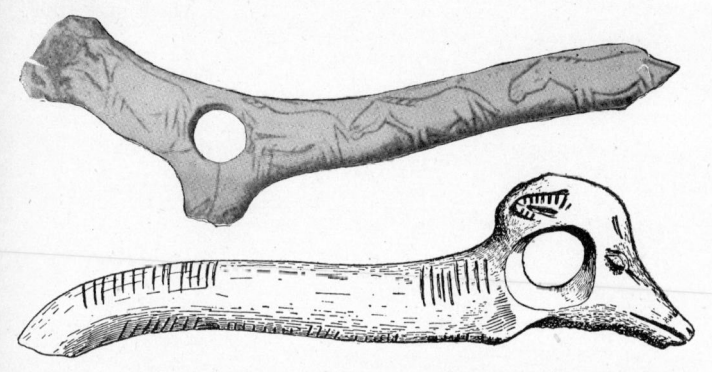

FIG. 34. Perforated staves of reindeer horn (after the Abbé Breuil).

of Spain, and it is true that there is good reason for doing so. On the other hand, if this practice is adopted, we have no general term for contemporary and very similar cultures which we meet with in other parts of the world. Besides this some implements of typical Magdalenian form, using this term in its restricted sense, have been found recently at Creswell Crags in Derbyshire and in the Mendip caves. It will perhaps be simplest to call all industries Magdalenian which immediately follow the Solutrean, remembering, however, that many of the characters described, such as those given above, apply only to the south-west European series, while those elsewhere are more like a developed Aurignacian, and show distinctive characters in different regions. They occur in some regions which show no traces of Solutrean culture.

In this broader sense, Magdalenian industries have been found from northern Spain across France to Belgium and the British Isles, to the north of Switzerland, Germany, and eastward as far at any rate as Austria and Poland. A somewhat similar industry, though possibly of later date, has been found in Siberia, chiefly in the Yenesei valley.

It is usually thought that during the period of Solutrean domination many of the Aurignacians fled to the fastnesses of the Pyrenees or other mountain regions, where flint was relatively scarce, and where they were, from lack of this material, compelled to develop an industry of bone and horn. On the departure of the Solutreans they returned to their old hunting grounds, but in the meantime the forests had grown up, so that they developed as isolated communities, having few, if any, relations with one another, in different parts of the Eurasiatic continent.

BOOKS

BURKITT, M. *Prehistory* (Cambridge, 1921 and 1925).
MACALISTER, R. A. S. *A Text-book of European Archaeology* (1921).
OBERMAIER, H. *Fossil Man in Spain* (Newhaven and Oxford, 1924).
SOLLAS, W. J. *Ancient Hunters* (London, 1924).
MACCURDY, G. G. *Human Origins* (2 vols., New York and London, 1925).

5
Early Types of Modern Man

WITH the passing of the Würm Ice Age the types of men occurring in western Europe change as remarkably as do the types of implements. Though we may think we can find indications of a transition from Mousterian to Aurignacian implements, there is certainly a very marked change in the physical type of man occurring at this period. We feel, therefore, that we must assume immigration to be the source of the new population. The elements of the new population must thus have had histories elsewhere, prior to their arrival in West Europe; some may have arrived via the Loess zone and some from Africa across still-persisting landbridges, but even if a group arrived by one or other of these routes, it need not have been quite homogeneous.

A notable feature of the hunters and artists of the later parts of the Old Stone Age is their diversity among themselves, a diversity so marked that the fashionable use of the term Cro-Magnon Race for all of them is very misleading and unfortunate. None the less, all are much nearer to the men of to-day than were their predecessors. They no longer have the great snout-like jaw projection, they walked more nearly erect though only some had quite attained this posture, their brains are usually larger than those of most of the earlier types and, in all cases, show a higher grade of organization. Some anthropologists have emphasized very strongly the contrasts between the Aurignacian immigrants and their Neanderthal predecessors in Europe and have suggested separate descent of the two sets from pre-human ancestors. Such views are probably exaggerated, but we have not yet gained much light on the problem of the time, place, and circumstances of the divergence of Neanderthal and 'Modern' Man; it may have been very early and was probably outside Europe. Modern man is in all probability not a descendant of Neanderthal man.

Generally speaking, both the absolute and the relative length of the skull is high in the types we are considering; the former often reaches or overtops 200 mm., especially in the earlier subjects, even though we have not here anything like the great frontal torus or overgrown brow-ridges of Neanderthal Man. In other words a marked growth in length of the brain case is a feature of these types, and we should consider with this the fact that the capacity of the brain case is often very great. We may take it that these men show a growth of the brain case greater than that of their predecessors, and that this growth has occurred mainly at the bone junctions or sutures going across the skull and comparatively little on the great bone junction of the median line, or the sagittal suture as it is called. This median line is still the first of the skull sutures to fuse in modern subjects and it would seem to have fused early in those days. This early fusion gave a much needed firmness to the attachment of the great jaw-muscles, the temporal muscles, which is still needed by people who from an early age use their jaws to tear flesh-food. There is much evidence of strong temporal muscles, pulling down the sides of the skull and so leaving in some cases a median ridge; the frequent projection of the cheek-bones is a noteworthy confirmation of this point, as are the strong back parts of the lower jaw. Brow ridges do occur in some subjects, but there are individuals without them and they are relatively weak in women. Another relic of the past, still found in some of the skulls under consideration, is the forward projection of the mouth; it is noteworthy in skulls Nos. 1 and 2 described in the appendix.[1]

[1] See p. 71.

Still another of these presumedly old features is the low broad orbit found in some of the skulls. In some the nose is small and broad, in others narrower and more prominent. Nos. 1 and 2 have feeble chins; these vary in the other subjects.

Comparing these early types, especially Nos. 1–26, with average European longheads of later times, we should note that the more modern people would show more general growth

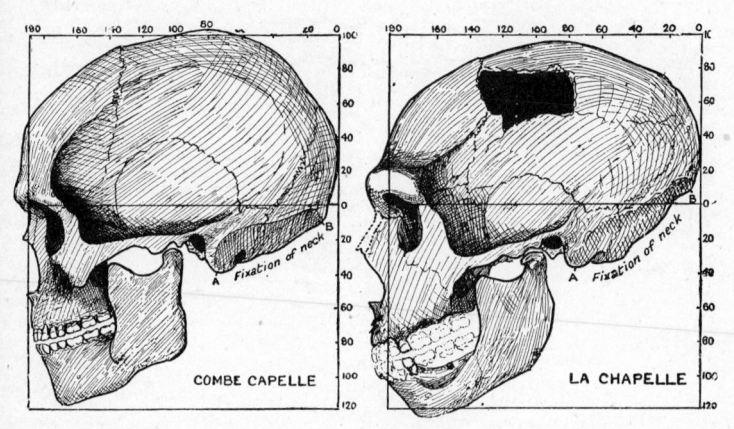

FIG. 35. Profiles of Upper Palaeolithic and Neanderthal man (after Keith).

of the skull with less special growth in length; in other words the cephalic index, or percentage ratio of breadth to length, runs higher now even in longheaded types. The head to-day is generally less highly ridged, the cheek-bones and jaws are more moderate; only a few types have marked brow ridges, and only in exceptional individuals does the mouth project forwards. The modern nose is usually like that of the narrowest of these old ones, and the orbits are now almost universally high and narrow. Generally we may put this down to a diminution of jaws and jaw muscles and a related narrowing of the face with attendant sharpening of the profile.

If we look upon the early skulls listed in the appendix as subjects at a fairly early stage in the process of evolution towards more modern features, we may next ask what can have been the circumstances which have favoured evolution in the direction indicated. Here, in the first place, we notice that Aurignacian man must have had a better developed society than his predecessors, that he had more freedom of initiative and also energy to devote to his remarkable artistic creations. We get an impression of communities perhaps with bases to which they were apt to return. Their implements, hearths, and hands suggest that already they prepared their food to a considerable extent before putting it into their mouths; this would be specially true for the preparation of food by the mothers for the babies. That, in the earlier stages, children were much desired seems fairly indicated. Putting these thoughts together one may suggest that somehow the Aurignacian peoples of Europe had somewhere learned more of the art of infant-welfare than had their predecessors. Delay in the closing of the bone junctions or sutures seems the inevitable result, and from this comes increased growth of the brain cavity and growth of the brain; this is especially so with better assured food supplies for the infants, the longer close association of children with their mothers and general social intercourse, with all the educational possibilities which that ensured.

The people of the Aurignacian Age are thus at an early stage of a remarkable process of evolution, and we may for the present look upon the various subjects studied as showing variant possibilities of this process. Nos. 1 and 2 seem earlier than any others. They could not walk erect, their mouths

FIG. 36. The Grimaldi skeletons (after Verneau).

projected strongly forwards, their noses were lowly in character. They have been said to be negroid, but this should not be over-emphasized. They, and some modern inhabitants of Africa, especially to the south-east of the Sudan, show features which also occur in a number of other stocks. It would be wiser to say that they retain ancient traits in a special degree.

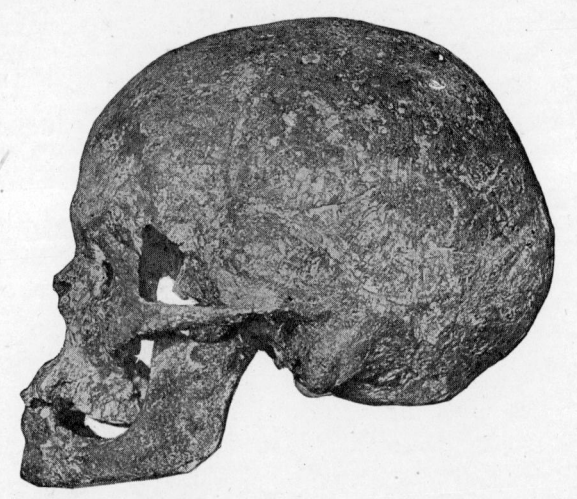

FIG. 37. The Grimaldi skull. (Photograph by the Abbé Villeneuve.)

The absence of brow ridges may, however, be said to suggest a link with some of the African peoples who have decidedly ancient features. It is almost beyond doubt that a modified form of the type of Nos. 1 and 2 occurs not infrequently in the poor quarters of Mediterranean towns and in many parts of North Africa. We may call it the lower Grimaldi type. Menghin has recently suggested that this type may have been associated with the early stages of East Spanish Art (see p. 87), but this seems very doubtful.

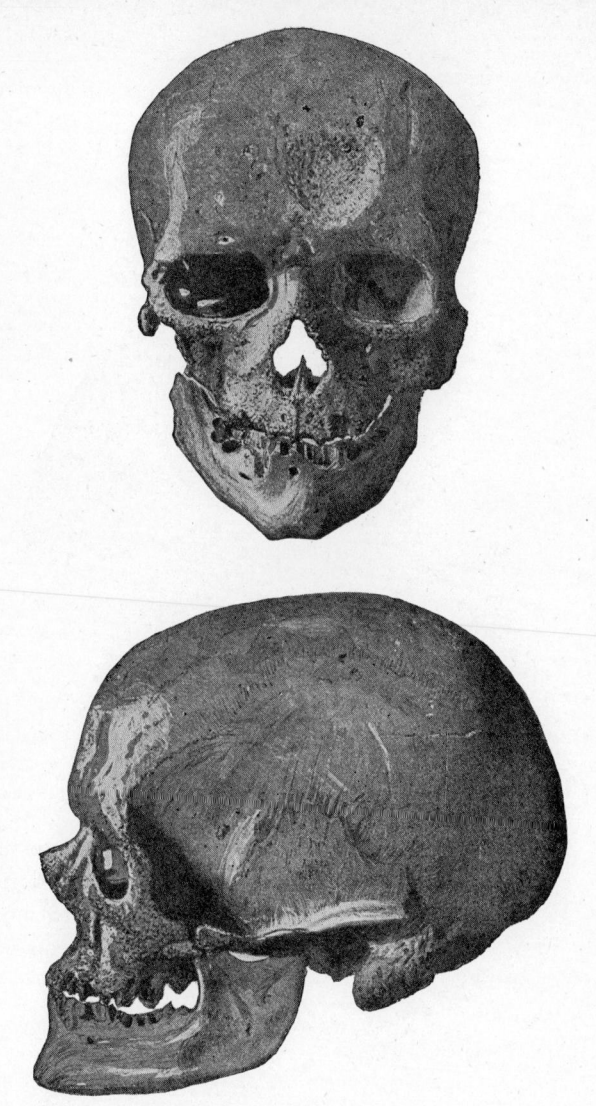

FIG. 38. The Old Man of Cro-Magnon (after Lartet and Christy).

Nos. 3, 4, 5, and 7 seem like one another and have been considered a 'race-type'. They were tall and appear to have stood erect; they had large brains. The skulls show less growth in height and, to make up, their breadth is greater, but the jaws and their muscles and consequently the cheek-bones, too, are very strong. The face is short and broad, with eye sockets low and the nose narrow and prominent. The name 'Cro-Magnon race' has been used for this type, but it has also been widely misused, for it has been applied to the whole group, or to a large part of the group, of skulls under discussion in this chapter. The short wide face of this type sometimes, as in Nos. 9, 10, 15d, and 33b, goes with a high, even a high-ridged head, which may have strong brow ridges, a distinct inheritance we are inclined to associate with the next group.

Nos. 18, 19, 20, 21, 23, 24 illustrate another group from Moravia in which the height of the head is great, in fact about equal to the breadth; the cephalic index is low, the brow ridges are strong, the cheek-bones are fairly wide, while the mouth tends to project forward. It seems related to Nos. 1 and 2 in some ways, but the brow ridges are very different, the chin is better formed, and the forward projection of the mouth much less. The head-cover of No. 9 and to some extent of No. 10, as well as of No. 33b, shows links with this type, while some women's skulls from Grimaldi, Nos. 8 and 11, seem to link with it too. No. 30 has obvious connexions, but here again the nose and chin are sharpened. No. 6 represents the type fairly perfectly. This group, including No. 6, was called by Klaatsch the Aurignacian race, but this term could apply equally well to either of the other groups; moreover, it seems to be as much associated with the Solutrean phase of culture. We may call it provisionally the Combe Capelle, or perhaps better the Predmost type by way of contrast with the Cro-Magnon type. In using the name we may approve its extension to cover cases with some advance towards the modern European condition as regards the sharpening of the nose and chin, provided that the ridged head, the brows and other standard characters are still present. Menghin has recently adopted the name 'Brünn Race' for this type, but we prefer not to give a name from so imperfect a specimen (No. 18). Descriptions of a group of skulls from Predmost (23) are to be published shortly and that name may well become the most suitable for designating the type. Nos. 17, 24a and 24b seem linked with the above but lack the great height of the head.

In some cases, such as Nos. 27 and 32b, we have something related to the type just mentioned, but the height is a little reduced and the relative breadth a little increased. The cephalic indices here are 75 and 74·6 against 66·7, 68·1, 62-9, 73·1 in the more typical examples of the group. The skulls recently found at Solutré and said to be Aurignacian in date show the high head and the low and broad orbits as well as the chin of the type under discussion, but the skull is much broader, the brow ridges are not strong and the stature is usually great, being 69 in. and 72 in. in two cases. The nose is long and narrow and the chin well marked. In fact in many respects, except for the orbits, these people might pass for modern Europeans and, as with the latter, the cephalic index is relatively high because of lack of excessive growth of the skull in length. It is important to note that something near the Predmost or Combe Capelle type, of skull at least, at times somewhat modified, has survived far and wide. It occurs in many graves of later periods and is well known in remote corners of most of the continents at the present day. Collignon, with remarkable perspicacity, described both it and the

Cro-Magnon type from the modern population of the Dordogne years before the Combe Capelle skull had been discovered in that department.

The fact that some individuals, like Nos. 9, 10, and 15d, carry some characters which place them closer to those of the Combe Capelle or Predmost type and others which bring them near to the Cro-Magnon type, may be held to suggest hybridization of originally separate stocks. There is, however, danger in this view. If we suppose that the skulls under discussion do illustrate variants of early stages of a progress towards modern character, we may think of the individuals as showing different combinations of these characters and of the new characters as variant responses to the new circumstances of growth indicated above.

In the course of time the human jaw has undergone such reduction that the Cro-Magnon type is no longer recognizable save in a few spots. The Predmost or Combe Capelle type, however, with its longer face is on the whole nearer to modern types, but when it survives it almost always does so with reduced height of the head, sharpened nose and chin and reduction of the forward projection of the mouth, while the orbits are now higher and narrower and the cheek-bones may be mildened considerably.

In discussing the skulls in groups we have omitted references to those from Solutré listed after No. 33. Of these Series I, Nos. v and viii are near the Combe Capelle type, save for a sharpening of the nose and chin; they approach modern conditions also in the orbits. Much the same may be said of Series II, No. i. Series I, Nos. i and perhaps iii seem possible forerunners of the broad-headed types of later times, while Series II, No. iii suggests the Cro-Magnon type but with the cheek-bones reduced. The subjects described after No. 33

all seem to show tendencies towards modern character in some way or another and there is not complete certainty about their real period, at least in the case of Series II, but they are clearly related to Nos. 15a–e, which are said to be of Aurignacian date.

It will be seen that we hesitate to suggest that we are dealing with different races of diverse origins and migrations, as has often been done. It may be that evidence for such a supposition will be found in the course of time. For the present, however, it seems easier to look upon the variant types as variant responses to changes in the conditions of growth, as has been suggested. These changes in the conditions of growth, once established, operate generation after generation, and they are changes that mean less 'roughing it' for the babies. If the old conditions were re-established it is therefore probable that the babes would die rather than that they would show reversion to the old characters. We should be careful not to commit ourselves for the present to the view that the variant responses mentioned above are responses to Aurignacian conditions in Europe; they may date back to earlier times elsewhere. There is no suggestion that they are changes which

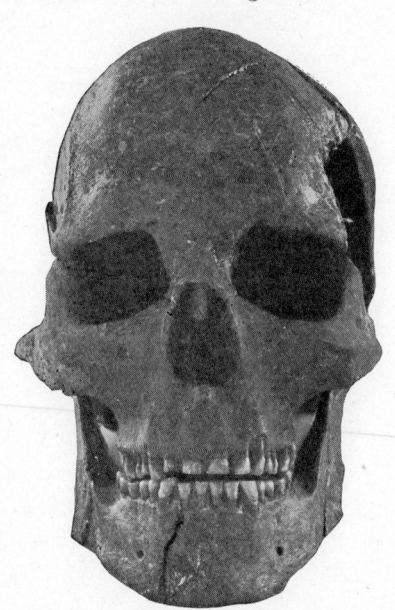

FIG. 39. The Combe Capelle skull (after Hauser).

occurred in originally Neanderthal-like ancestors; for such an opinion there would seem to be no evidence whatever. The main suggestion is that we are dealing with cases of increased growth of the cubic capacity of the brain, an increased growth which in early days was subject to the governing condition that a firm basis on the skull for the strong temporal muscles had still to be established definitely at a fairly early period of life.

It is gratifying to gather from a number of recent references to the subject in books and papers that the view, upheld for a number of years by Professor Fürst, Professor Klaatsch, the late Professor Giuffrida-Ruggeri, and the writers of this book, is gaining ground. This view is that the people of the later Palaeolithic Age, apart from the lower Grimaldi type, could not usefully be labelled 'Cro-Magnon' as a whole. The Combe Capelle type seems to have left more, albeit modified, descendants. It is only provisionally named from the French skull, for it is a type that seems to be more characteristic of Central Europe and, when more is known of a collection of skulls from Czecho-Slovakia (23), we may perhaps find ourselves far better able to deal with the subject. For the present our hope must be to provide hypotheses that will stimulate unprejudiced observation of characters in any new finds, and it is especially for this reason that we deprecate the now fast diminishing tendency to make the name 'Cro-Magnon' cover a number of variants.

APPENDIX

CATALOGUE OF THE BETTER-KNOWN SKULLS AND SKELETONS OF THE UPPER PALAEOLITHIC AGE

Aurignacian

1. GRIMALDI, GROTTE DES ENFANTS. LOWER LAYER. Old woman. Stature 1590 (6¾″), L. 191, B. 131, C.I. 68·6, H. 129 ?, Bz. 129, Orbit 27/38, i. e. low and broad, Nose 28/44 i. e. broad and small, Cubic capacity 1375. Ratios of Radius/humerus and Tibia/femur high, as in many early types and their survivors. Pelvis shows early characters. Walked with knees bent. Skull has steep median ridge, lower margin of nose guttered, brow ridges not developed, strong cheek-bones, face short and flat, chin very weak. Each of the three molars has five tubercles, as against 4, with sometimes a fifth in the first two in most modern men except the Australians. Very early.

2. THE SAME. Young man (immature). St. 1560 (61½″), L. 192, B. 133, C.I. 69·3, H. 137 ?, Bz. 130 ?, Orbit 26/39 i. e. low and broad, Nose ? 25/46 i. e. broad and small, C.C. 1580. Other characters as in No. 1. Very early.

3. CRO-MAGNON, DORDOGNE. Old man. S. 1800 (71″), L. 202–3, B. 149–152, C.I. 73·7–74·8, H. 132–140, Bz. 143, Orbit 27/41–44 i. e. low and broad, Nose 23/51 or 27/57 i. e. relatively narrow and prominent, C.C. 1590. Ratio of arm to stature small. Skull has median line relatively low, brow ridges moderate, cheek-bones very strong, face short and broad, chin very strong.

4 and 5. THE SAME. Man and woman. Presumably as No. 3. Also fragments of two others.

6. COMBE CAPELLE, DORDOGNE. Man, middle-aged. S. 1550 (62″), L. 201, B. 134, C.I. 66·7, H. 137, Bz.?, Orbit low and broad, Nose rather broad and small, C.C. 1440. Skull has steep median ridge, brow ridges well developed, strong cheek-bones, rather long face, chin weaker than in Nos. 3–5 but stronger than in Nos. 1 and 2. Contracted burial.

7. GRIMALDI, GROTTE DES ENFANTS. Man. S. 1890 (74½″), L. 198 ?, B. 151, C.I. 76·3, H. 133 ?, Bz. 155 ?, Orbit 30/45 i. e. low and broad and rectangular, Nose ? 29/51 i. e. broad and of moderate

size, C.C. 1715–1775. Median line of skull low and not ridged, brow moderate, cheek-bones very strong, face moderate length, no forward projection of mouth, chin strong. Extended burial. On the whole closely akin to Nos. 3–5.

8. THE SAME. Woman. Broken skeleton. May be of later date. Skull evidently long, face long, brow ridges fairly strong, orbits low and wide, mouth projects forward, chin strong. Stature probably 1530 (62").

9. GRIMALDI, BARMA GRANDE. Male, may show posthumous deformation. S. 1880 (74"), L. 211, B. 134 ?, C.I. 63 ?, Orbit 29/48 ? i. e. low and broad, C.C. high. Median line of skull obviously high, brow strong, nose relatively narrow, cheek-bones broad and face wide and short, hardly any forward projection of mouth. Face like Nos. 3–5, head more like No. 6.

10. THE SAME. Male. May show posthumous deformations. S. 1770 (70"), L. 206, B. 142 ?, C.I. 69–71·4, H. 158 ?, Bz. 152, Orbit 30/43 i. e. low and broad, Nose 25/53 rather narrow, C.C. 1900 ?. Skull very high, brow fairly strong, cheek-bones strong, face wide and fairly short, little forward projection of mouth, well-marked chin. Face like Nos. 3–5, head doubtful, but in any case its height differentiates it from Nos. 3–5.

11. THE SAME. Female. Young. L. 190, B. 136, C.I. 71·6, Bz. 130, Orbit 31/42 i. e. fairly low and broad, Nose 25/54 i. e. moderately broad and fairly prominent. Median line of skull fairly high, brows weak, cheek-bones strong, face long, marked projection forward of mouth, well-marked chin. In several points akin to No. 6 rather than to Nos. 3–5.

12. THE SAME. Male. Young. L. 177 ?, B. 135, C.I. 76·3, Bz. 134, Orbit 31/42 i. e. moderately low and broad. Much posthumous deformation. Face broad, cheek-bones prominent.

13. THE SAME. Skeleton in the Museum at Mentone. Male. L. L. 194, B. 140, C.I. 72·2. Brows very strong, face moderate, chin strong, mouth projects forward.

13a. GRIMALDI, GROTTE DU CAVILLON. Tall, very long-headed with broad face and low orbits and narrow nose.

Note also parts of two skeletons from Baousso da Torre, Grimaldi, which are tall and long-headed. These are presumably akin to Nos. 3–5.

14. PAVILAND, SOUTH WALES. Probably a woman. Skull missing. S. (inferred) 1700–1735 (67″–68″). Proportions of leg bones as in many early types.
15. SOLUTRÉ (1921–4 excavations).
    a. Man. Young. S. 1830 (72″), C.I. 79·3, Bz. 143, C.C. 1690. Head very high, brow ridges not strong, cheek-bones strong, face fairly long, nose long and narrow, orbits low and broad, well-marked chin. (No. 2 of publ. accounts.)
    b. Man. Young. S. 1750 (69″), L. 184, B. 146, C.I. 79·3, C.C. 1600. Other characters much like a. (No. 3 of publ. accounts.)
    c. Woman. Young. S. 1550 (61″), C.I. 77·7. (No. 1 of publ. accounts.)
    d. Man. Middle-aged. S. 1670–1700 (66″–67″), C.I. 77·9. Head high, face broad and short, cheek-bones fairly strong, orbits low and broad, nose fairly broad. (No. 4 of publ. accounts.)
    e. Woman. Young. S. 1530–1550 (60″–61″), C.I. 83·2. Head moderately high, face broad and short, cheek-bones strong, orbits fairly high and moderately narrow, fairly broad nose, strong jaw. Conceivably rather later in date. (No. 5 of publ. accounts.)
15. a–e are clearly not to be grouped too closely with any of the others mentioned above. It is thought by a few anthropologists that these skeletons are of a later date, but became buried under material derived from a landslide. This is usually deemed improbable.
16. ENZHEIM, NEAR STRASBOURG. Details do not appear to have been published.
17. MECHTA EL ARBI, French North Africa.
    a. Male, L. 193, B. 148, C.I. 76·7, H. 122 ?, Orbit 35/42, Nose, 30/52, Bz. 144.
    b. Male, L. 192, B. 141, C.I. 73·44, Nose ? 28/57.
    c. Female, L. 178 ?, B. 141, C.I. ? 80.

Strong glabella and brow ridges, retreating forehead, broad nose, stature low.

Solutrean

18. BRÜNN. Man. Broken on right side of skull, so that measurements are largely inferred. L. 204 ?, B. 139 ?, C.I. 68·1, H. ca. 140. Head very high, brow ridges strong. Resembles No. 6.
19. BRÜNN. Woman. L. 192, B. 139, C.I. 72·3.

20. BRÜNN. Much broken. Probably a man. L. 190–201, B. 139, C.I. 62–69. Head rather high, brow ridges strong. Resembles No. 6. Nos. 18–20 may be Aurignacian in date.

21. BRÜX. Male. L. 190–195, B. 130–135, C.I. probably nearly 70. Another estimate by Sergi is L. 201, B. 124, C.I. 61·7. Somewhat doubtful.

22. PREDMOST. Boy, about twelve years of age. L. 176, B. 134, C.I. 76·1, H. 120, Orbit 30/38 i. e. moderate, Nose 20/40 i. e. moderate, mouth projects forwards, C.C. 1335.

23. THE SAME. Foot of a cliff, edge of loess, 14 skeletons still undescribed. Provisional description of two :

a 1. Male, L. 203, B. 146, C.I. 71·9, high, strong brow ridges and glabella, forehead high but retreating, skull with median line fairly marked, orbits low and wide, nose strong, rather long and narrow, chin prominent, mouth projects slightly, palate large, brain case rather large.

a 2. Female, L. 193, B. 143, C.I. 74, high, brow ridges not very marked, forehead high, rising steeply, orbits relatively higher and less wide than in the man, mouth does not project forward, nose relatively broader than in the man, chin fairly developed, brain case very large for a woman.

24. LAUTSCH. L. 193, B. 141, C.I. 73·1, H. 140, Bz. 135, Orbit 29/40 i. e. low and fairly broad, Nose 24/50 i. e. moderately long and narrow. Head high, brows well marked, cheek-bones strong, mouth projects forward. Resembles No. 6 in some points. Some writers give this a Magdalenian date.

24a. LAUTSCH V. L. 206, B. 149, C.I. 72·3, Auric. H. ? 98. Brow ridges strong, separate. Head apparently very low.

24b. LAUTSCH VI. L. 201, Dolichocephalic. Brow ridges strong and connected by strong glabella. Head apparently very low.

25. HUSSOWITZ (near Brünn). Age questioned. L. 197, B. 145, C.I. 73·6, Auric. H. 115–120, Orbit 31/42, Nose ?.

26. KLAUSE, NEU ESSING. Details do not appear to have been published.

26a. BALLAHÖHLE (MISKOLCZ, POLAND). Skeleton of an infant, said to be of type of 18–20.

Magdalenian

27. LA FAYE BRUNIQUEL. Man. L. 184, B. 138, C.I. 75·0, H. 133, Orbit 29/33·5 i. e. low but narrow. Small broad face, nose moderate, slight forward projection of the mouth, good chin.
28. THE SAME. Woman. C.I. estimated at 74. Head high, orbits moderate, nose narrow, face moderate.
29. LAUGERIE BASSE.
    - a. Back of skull, male.
    - b. Female ?. L. 179, B. 134, C.I. 74·9. Brow ridges almost nil.
    - c. Infant.
    - d. Man. L. 195, B. 146, C.I. 74·9. Brow fairly strong, face long.
30. CHANCELADE. Man. S. calculated at 1575 (62″), L. 193, B. 139, C.I. 72, H. 150, Bz. 140, Orbit 32/38 and 34/57 i. e. fairly high and fairly narrow, Nose 26/61 i. e. narrow and long, C.C. 1700. Skull very high, brow ridges moderate, cheek-bones moderate, face rather long, chin strong. Walked with knees bent, large hands and feet. Has some characters in common with No. 6, others not. Has been compared with Eskimo.
31. LE PLACARD. Fragmentary. C.I. probably about 80. Head high, brow ridges not strong, nose prominent.
32. SORDE. Several skeletons, of which we have details of two.
    - a. Male. L. 190, B. 140, C.I. 73·8, H. ?, Orbit 30·5/42 i. e. fairly high and narrow, Nose 22/53 i. e. narrow and fairly long.
    - b. Female. L. 184, B. 138, C.I. 74·6, H. 133, Bz. 130, Orbit 33/39 i. e. fairly high and narrow, Nose 24/53 i. e. fairly narrow and long, C.C. 1520.

    These may be comparable on the whole with Nos. 22 and 23.
33. OBERCASSEL, BONN, GERMANY.
    - a. Woman, aged 20. S. about 1550 (61″), C.I. 70. Head with fairly marked median ridge, fairly strong brow ridges, fairly strong cheek-bones, nose and orbits moderate, chin well formed.
    - b. Man, aged 40–50 years. S. about 1600 (63″), L. 195, B. 144, C.I. 74, Bz. 153, C.C. 1500. Head high with well-marked median ridge, very strong brow ridges, orbits fairly low and broad, very strong cheek-bones and short broad face, nose narrow, chin strong.

    Resembles Nos. 3–5 in face but No. 6 in stature, headform and cubic capacity of brain case.

Age uncertain. Said to be Upper Palaeolithic

I. SOLUTRÉ, FRANCE.
- Series I.
  - i. Male. L. 175, B. 145, C.I. 83·2, H. 133, Bz. 135, Orbits 30/42 i. e. fairly broad. Head with low but well-marked median ridge, brow ridges fairly well marked, nose fairly broad.
  - ii. Female. L. 180, B. 142, C.I. 79, H. 137, Bz. 131, Orbit 30/36 i. e. narrow. Brows rather well marked, strong chin, mouth projects forward.
  - iii. Male. L. 185, B. 149, C.I. 80·4, H. 140, Bz. 140, Orbit 35/38 i. e. high and narrow.
  - iv. Male. L. 193, B. 151, C.I. 73·6, H. 138, Bz. 150, Orbit 37/39 i. e. high and fairly narrow.
  - v. Male. L. 190, B. 140, C.I. 73·6, H. 138, Bz. 135, Orbit 29/37. Head high with median line moderately marked, brow ridges fairly strong, orbits low, cheek-bones moderate, nose rather narrow and prominent.
  - vi. Estimates only. L. 193, B. 145, C.I. 75·1.
  - vii. Estimates only. L. 200, B. 137, C.I. 68·5.
  - viii. Male. L. 190, B. 133, C.I. 70, H. 140, Bz. 133, Orbit 34/55 i. e. high and narrow. Head high, median ridge well marked, brows fairly well marked, nose narrow, strong chin.
- Series II.
  - i. Male. L. 190, B. 140, C.I. 73·2, H. 137, Bz. 130, Orbit 33/36 i. e. fairly high and narrow.
  - ii. Female. L. 188, B. ?, C.I. 69/1 ?, H. ?, Bz. ?, Orbit ?.
  - iii. Male. L. 188, B. 150, C.I. 79·6, H. 134, Bz. 132, Orbit 31/35 i. e. fairly high and quite narrow. Head not very high, chin strong.
  - iv. Male. L. 184, B. 148, C.I. 80·4, H. ?, Bz. 127, Orbit 33/38 i. e. fairly high.
- Series III. Measurements uncertain owing to fragmentary condition.

II. ALCOLEA, near Cordoba, Spain. L. 188, B. 135, C.I. 71·8. Height (not stated whether Basi-bregmatic or Auricular) 124, Supra-orbital torus said to be complete but not heavy. Chin indicated, teeth not very primitive. Age uncertain, but probably Pleistocene.

III. OUNDORY, R. VOLGA, GOVT. SAMARA, RUSSIA.
    (1) L. 177, B. 120, C.I. about 67·0, height of vault 88, strong glabella and supra-orbital ridges, retreating forehead, probably female, vault only.
    (2) L. 206, B. 132, C.I. 64·0, height of vault 102, very strong glabella and supra-orbital ridges, temporal ridge, forehead retreating, male, compared by Pavlov with Combe Capelle, &c

BOOKS

BOULE, M. *Fossil Man* (Edinburgh, 1923).
KEITH, A. *The Antiquity of Man* (London, 2nd Ed., 1925).
OBERMAIER, H. *Fossil Man in Spain* (Newhaven and London, 1924).

6

The Life and Thought of the Times

As we have seen, the men of the Upper Palaeolithic Age lived much in caves. During the long severe winters they must have spent a great deal of their time in these retreats, and even during the summer months, in spite of long expeditions in search of game, it seems probable that they returned to these homes at intervals, and perhaps left their wives and children there while they were absent on the chase. In such permanent abodes they left many of their belongings and the refuse of their meals, so that we have far more details from which to reconstruct a picture of their daily life than was the case when we were dealing with the men of the Lower and Middle Palaeolithic Ages.

Throughout all this time the inhabitants of Europe seem to have remained in the hunting stage and depended on the products of the chase for their food and for the raw materials of their clothing. The chase was the work of the men rather than of the women, who doubtless dressed the food and skins, and, with their children's help, collected berries and nuts. No satisfactory evidence has been produced to show that they cultivated any plants or grains, for, though an attempt was once made to show that plants were represented in the drawings which were made at the close of the period, all archaeologists are now agreed that these symbols are not intended to represent plants, still less plants under cultivation. It has been claimed, too, that they had tamed the horse, but the evidence for this is usually considered insufficient.

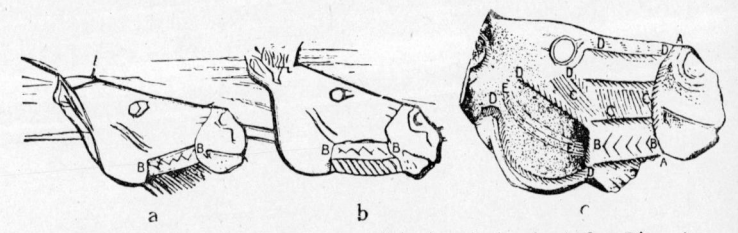

FIG. 40. Conventional sculpture of the horse's head. (After Piette.) The letters refer to statements in M. Piette's paper.

We have seen that the tools and weapons which they made were of many different types, and by no means of one material. It is true that flint is the raw material most often used, and that they had acquired a considerable skill in shaping these fragments according to their desires; but bone, which occurs sometimes though rarely in Mousterian deposits, became more and more frequently used as time went on, and was the most important raw material in Magdalenian times. It seems almost certain, too, that wood was also used, though no wooden objects of this date have been found; there is, however, ample evidence that, at any rate in the east of Spain, bows and arrows were in common use before the close of the period.

But what distinguishes this period in Europe most clearly

from those which had gone before is the art, painting, engraving, and sculpture, which had already reached a fairly high standard at the beginning of Aurignacian times, so much so that we must imagine that these modern men, who arrived in Europe after the maximum of the Würm glaciation, must have been familiar with these arts long before they set foot on European soil. The art is of two kinds: carvings on or out of stone, bone, or ivory, which the French call *Art mobilier*,

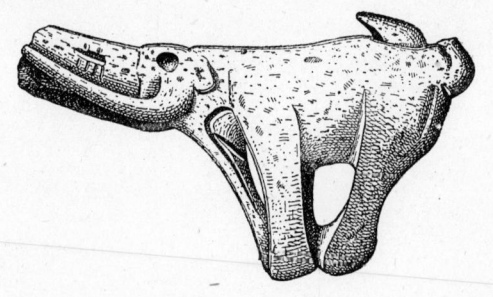

FIG. 41. Magdalenian dart-thrower of reindeer horn, representing a mammoth. (After de Mortillet.)

which has been translated 'mobiliary art', 'portable art', or 'home art', but which we prefer to call 'chattel art', and engravings and paintings on the cave walls, which are termed 'mural art'. There are, it is true, a few cases which do not come well under either heading, such as models in clay fixed to the floor; these are, however, usually included among the instances of chattel art.

Decorated chattels, which have been found in Late Palaeolithic deposits, are of various types; some have been carved in the round, some in high or low relief, while some are merely engravings in outline, with or without shading. They have been carved on or out of stone, bone, or ivory; those on bone are frequently ornaments on the objects of daily use, such as the handles of knives, or those strange objects known as arrow-straighteners or ' bâtons de commandement '. These decorated chattels bear almost invariably representations of human beings or animals, often very realistic, though towards the close of the period sometimes very much tylized. At the end of the

FIG. 42. Female statuette from the cave of Barma Grande. Aurignacian period. (After Reinach.)

period we meet with objects adorned with conventional ornament, which seems to have been evolved from highly stylized zoomorphic designs.

The representations of the human figure are found most commonly in Aurignacian deposits, and during the early part of this period they are usually in the round ; towards its close we find carvings in high relief more frequent. In Central Europe figures in the round have been found in deposits

The Life and Thought of the Times

which have been thought to belong to the Solutrean period, and several such figures have been claimed as of Solutrean workmanship. It is now, however, more generally believed that these represent a very late Aurignacian culture, which persisted in Moravia after the arrival of the Solutrean hunters in the plain of Hungary. In Magdalenian times the human figure is rarely represented, and among the few instances which have been noted are some engravings on arrow-

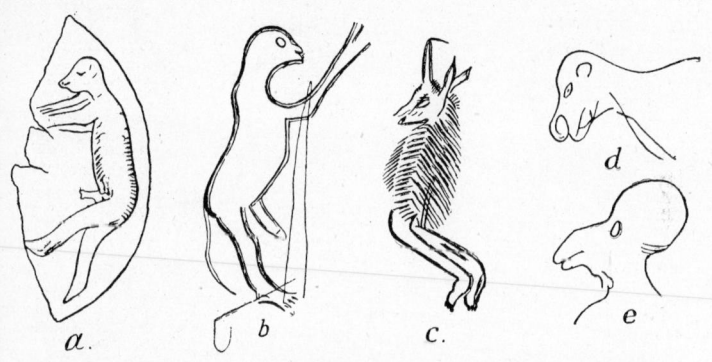

FIG. 43. Anthropomorphic design. (After Piette and Breuil.)
a. Engraving on bone, Mas d'Azil. *b, d, e.* Cave grotesques. *c.* Human figure masked as chamois, Abri Mège.

straighteners of human beings in animal masks; these may, however, represent animals somewhat anthropomorphized. Broadly speaking, we find a steady movement from the representation of human figures in the round to stylized or conventional figures engraved on objects of everyday use, although the earlier form arose or survived in Central Europe at a later date than in southern France.

The representation of animal forms seems to follow much the same evolution. Figures in the round are, however, relatively rarer, and date only, it would seem, from Upper

Aurignacian times. Realistic representations of animals survived well into Magdalenian times, and show signs of stylization only in the closing phase of the period. True conventionalization does not occur with frequency until Mesolithic times, though there is some evidence of its occurrence in the closing phase of the Magdalenian period.

That late palaeolithic man had discovered the art of modelling in clay was apparent when in October 1912 Count Bégouen discovered in the cave of Tuc d'Audoubert, near Montesquieu, Ariège, two figures of bison, about two feet long, made of this material. They were found at the far end of the cave, leaning against a boulder which had fallen from the roof; two others, unfinished, were found close by. Other figures in clay have been found recently not far from St. Girons, but the number discovered so far is small; this is probably due to the perishable nature of the material. For palaeolithic man had failed to discover that by baking the clay he could render it practicably indestructible, and so such objects have usually perished. This failure on his part doubtless accounts for the fact that he did not succeed in discovering the advantages of pottery for domestic use.

It is, however, by their mural art that the men of the late Palaeolithic Age are best known, and this art shows a steady progress from the beginning until near to the end, when, after the climax has been reached, a rapid degeneration sets in. These mural decorations are, in nearly all cases, realistic pictures of animals, sometimes engraved on the surface of the rock, sometimes painted upon it, and sometimes a combination of both techniques; the painting is both monochrome and polychrome.

During Lower and Middle Aurignacian times we find very simple designs; rows of dots, spiral tracings, and silhouettes of hands, of which more later on. These are followed by primitive pictures of animals traced with the finger upon the wet clay adhering to the cave walls. Then come deeply engraved pictures, and a few paintings in simple linear outline in red or black pigment. In Upper Aurignacian times the

FIG. 44. Two bison, modelled in clay, from the cave of Tuc d'Audoubert. (After the Count de Bégouen.)

drawing is better, and the simple engraved outlines have a more realistic appearance. The painted pictures are also more elaborate, for the modelling of the animal is frequently shown by shaded colour, sometimes by groups of lines or rows of dots.

It was formerly believed that no art existed during the Solutrean interlude in the areas affected by it, and that the invaders of this time were a barbaric hunting people, keen on the chase, but lacking in artistic feelings. Recently, however, a few works of art, which must be unquestionably classed as belonging to this period, have been discovered, though full details have not yet been published. There has been in consequence a tendency to look upon the Solutrean hunters in a different light. Seeing, however, that works of art belonging

FIG. 45. Drawing in red of an elephant in the cave of Castillo, near Santander. First phase of the Aurignacian period. (After Alcaldi de Rio, Breuil, and Sierra.)

to this period are very few in number, and show, apparently, no very distinctive character, it is permissible still to adhere to the former view, and to consider these works of art as of Aurignacian workmanship though executed in Solutrean times.

In Early Magdalenian times engraving reached its highest pitch, and the paintings still continued to be in black with an increased amount of shading. Sometimes engraving and painting were combined, with or without shading. In Middle

Magdalenian times engraving was going out of fashion, and such examples as have been found are of very small dimensions and only very lightly incised. On the other hand the art of painting advanced, and we get beautiful polychrome pictures of animals, sometimes of full size. In Late Magdalenian times there is a sudden decline in the technique, the outlines are frequently inaccurately drawn, though there are still a few fine polychrome paintings reminiscent of the best period.

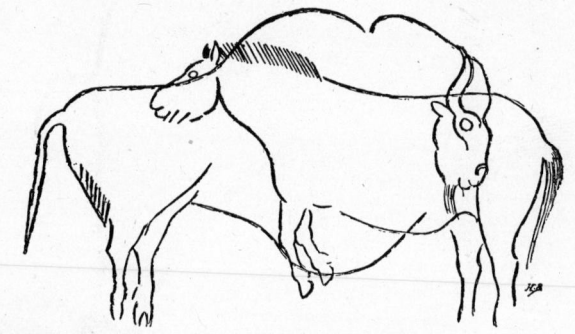

FIG. 46. Engraving of a bison and horse, from Les Combarelles. (After Breuil.)

After this engraving ceases there are no realistic pictures of animals, and we have nothing but a number of conventional signs.

It is noticeable that with a few exceptions the pictures are all of animals, and for the most part of animals which were hunted for food. The animals are drawn singly, and there is no grouping into scenes. The only cases of human representation occur towards the close of the period, and one of these is of a man disguised in the skin and head of an animal, from the cave of Les Trois Frères; this is believed to be a representation of a sorcerer or witch-doctor.

The silhouettes of hands, dating from Early Aurignacian times, are of two kinds. In one case the hand was placed against the wall and paint sprayed around it, while in the other the hand was smeared with pigment and laid upon the

Fig. 47. Painting of an ox in the cave of Font-de-Gaume.
(After Capitan, Breuil, and Peyrony.)

wall. It is curious to note that in several cases some of the fingers lack one or more digits, which seems to show that mutilation, by the removal of joints of digits, a practice in vogue in more than one modern primitive tribe, was customary among the Early Aurignacian folk.

But in Spain, especially in the eastern part of the peninsula, there occurs another and totally different type of art, which is known as East Spanish Art. This, as far as is known at present, consists of mural art only. The pictures, which are

FIG. 48. Hands, silhouetted against a colour, from the cave of Castillo. (After Breuil.)

usually very small, with the figures only a few inches across, are found in rock shelters rather than in caves, and represent, not single figures of animals, but hunting scenes in which both animals and human beings are depicted. The style is in many respects different, and though the figures, especially those of the men, are drawn with little attempt at accuracy, the pictures have much vigour, and usually express rapid motion. In many respects these scenes resemble more the paintings of the Bushmen on the rocks in South Africa than the work of the palaeolithic artists of the caves of France and North Spain, yet even to the latter they show certain well-defined resemblances, especially in the treatment of animal subjects. They also show considerable divergences among themselves in the representation of the human figure.

For long the age of these paintings was much in dispute, and there was a tendency in some quarters to consider them as the works of neolithic man, even though they might belong to the earlier half of that period. Now, however, after more careful study, Professor Obermaier has adduced what seems to be conclusive evidence of their palaeolithic date. He has pointed out that on some sites a number of drawings are found superimposed, so that a chronological series can be made out. This series shows changes exactly parallel to those of late palaeolithic art; moreover, upon the top of some of them appear those conventional signs which we have been led to associate with early mesolithic art. The animals, too, are the same species as those depicted in the French caves.

We may now consider their Palaeolithic Age as established, and see in these paintings the work of those Capsian invaders who crossed the Straits of Gibraltar from North Africa only a little after Aurignacian man had arrived in the south of France. Their art had sprung from the same sources, was actuated by the same motives, but had developed on a parallel course. Though no decorated chattels have been found, we must not yet assume that none existed, for their paintings have, so far, mainly been found under overhanging rocks on sites which were not used as regular habitations.

FIG. 49. The Stag Hunt from the 'Cueva del Mas d'en Josep'.

The successive styles, as distinguished by Breuil and Obermaier, are six in number. The first, termed the first phase of Early Capsian, is equivalent in date to the later phases of the Aurignacian, and is characterized by small figures of primitive type and incorrectly drawn. The second phase, which is thought to be coeval with Solutrean, exhibits monochrome linear paintings of a more realistic type.

The next style, known as the first phase of the Late Capsian,

FIG. 50. War Dance of Archers, from 'Cueva del Civil', Castellón.

seems to be equivalent to the Early Magdalenian of France, and shows larger pictures, still monochrome, but in very good style and technique. Towards the close of this phase we find linear drawings with some shading. The second phase, equivalent to the Middle Magdalenian, has monochrome pictures, partly shaded; and the third phase, contemporary with the Late Magdalenian, has polychrome and semi-polychrome paintings. The fourth phase, which belongs rather to the beginning of the mesolithic period, shows great decadence and conventionalization.

The paintings from different sites show considerable variation, especially in the treatment of the human figure; this is,

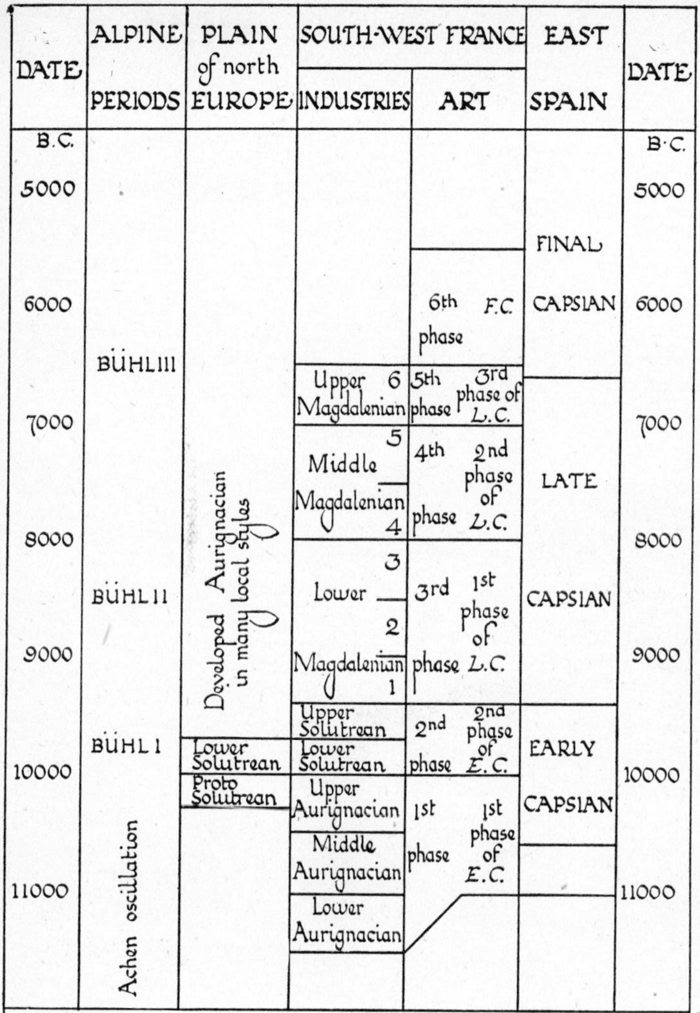

DATE	ALPINE PERIODS	PLAIN of north EUROPE	SOUTH-WEST FRANCE INDUSTRIES	ART	EAST SPAIN	DATE
B.C.						B.C.
5000						5000
					FINAL CAPSIAN	
6000				6th phase F.C.		6000
	BÜHL III		Upper Magdalenian 6	5th phase	3rd phase of L.C.	
7000			5	4th phase	2nd phase of L.C.	LATE	7000
		Developed Aurignacian in many local styles	Middle Magdalenian 4			
8000			3			8000
	BÜHL II		Lower Magdalenian 2	3rd phase	1st phase of L.C.	CAPSIAN	
9000			1				9000
			Upper Solutrean	2nd phase	2nd phase of E.C.	EARLY CAPSIAN	
10000	BÜHL I	Lower Solutrean Proto Solutrean	Lower Solutrean				10000
			Upper Aurignacian	1st phase	1st phase of E.C.		
	Achen oscillation		Middle Aurignacian				
11000			Lower Aurignacian				11000

Fig. 51. Chart of the industries & art of the Upper Palæolithic Periods.

Note. The chart reads, in order of time, from the bottom upwards.

perhaps, partly due to varieties in the style of dress. As these pictures represent scenes, and human figures are almost as numerous as those of animals, we can glean much information as to the customs, clothes, and weapons of the people, but we must be careful not to take it for granted that identical customs prevailed north of the Pyrenees.

As to the motives which led to the production of these artistic displays there has been some difference of opinion. Some have suggested merely *joie de vivre*, others the need of some occupation during periods of enforced idleness; but the majority of anthropologists see behind these paintings a religious motive. If this be so, and the main idea of drawing a bison is to express the wish that there be many bisons, and that the pictures were drawn in the hope that by sympathetic magic their kind would multiply, we must imagine that the desires of the earliest Aurignacian immigrants to France aimed at an increase in the population, and that they wished for more children from their fat and fruitful women. By degrees this desire waned, and the population began to multiply as fast as the food supply warranted, till at length the desire was only for more beasts to eat, and the only human representations were those of the medicine-man who helped to perform the magic. Among the Capsian men in East Spain the great wish all through was for ' good hunting '.

Menghin has recently suggested that the East Spanish art may be connected with the Grimaldi type, the art of mural painting in south-west France and north-west Spain with the Cro-Magnon type and the sculptures and modelling in the round with the Combe Capelle, or, as he prefers to call it, the Brünn type. These suggestions seem to go rather beyond the evidence. In our view, the region of south-west France and north-west Spain was a focus wherein human types and their cultures mingled; to this Menghin would agree. In such foci taboos would be relaxed and human initiative would be

Fig. 52. Female figures from the principal shelter at Alpera, Albacete, painted in dark red.

liberated. Thus we get, not only cross fertilization of culture and exchanges of traditions, but development of new ideas in many directions. Venice, Florence, and Bruges, with their influence on the development of medieval art, are instances of such foci.

The pictures, especially those from the east of Spain, show us that in these days both men and women were sometimes clothed, and occasionally wore curious head-dresses. They tell us, too, that the men combined to hunt the animals needed for food, while their women folk sometimes looked on and danced ritual dances. We learn, too, that, in Magdalenian times at least, the Capsian men were armed with bows and arrows, and there is some reason for believing that their neighbours in France were not behind them in this respect.

The evidence at our disposal goes to show that frequently, we might almost say usually, care was taken to dispose of the bodies of the dead in a seemly way. These folk seem to have buried rather than burned their dead, and laid them out usually in an extended position, though a crouched attitude was sometimes adopted. The dead were buried with the weapons and implements they had used during life, and in some cases, notably in that of the mother and son in the lower layer in the Grotte des Enfants, the dead were buried in their clothes and with their shell or bone ornaments. A remarkable rite, which persisted in some parts until fairly recent times, was that of covering the bones with red ochre. It has been supposed that this ochre was laid on the body before burial, though this has been disputed; it is even possible that the custom of painting the body red was one practised during life.

All these rites indicate a feeling of respect for the departed, and the presence of the possessions of the deceased in the grave has led to the assertion that these men of the Upper Palaeolithic Age held a belief in a life after death; this may be so, but an alternative explanation is that it would be unlucky to appropriate the effects of the deceased, and so they were buried with the corpse. Some religious ideas they had undoubtedly, for their paintings are best explained as instances of sympathetic magic. Some oval pendants of bone or stone, found at Laugerie Basse and Laugerie Haute, amongst other places, have been interpreted as 'bull-roarers', magic implements used by primitive tribes in many parts of the world.

BOOKS

BURKITT, M. *Prehistory* (Cambridge, 1921 and 1925).
MACALISTER, R. A. S. *A Text-book of European Archaeology* (1921).
MACCURDY, G. G. *Human Origins* (2 vols., New York and London, 1925).
OBERMAIER, H. *Fossil Man in Spain* (Newhaven and Oxford, 1924).
SOLLAS, W. J. *Ancient Hunters* (London, 1924).

7
Palaeolithic Survivals

WE have seen that during the last phases of the Magdalenian period the climate was becoming moister, for the storm zone, which had hitherto swept across the Mediterranean, had shifted to a more northerly course; as a result, the open grass lands were becoming covered with trees. The pine appeared first, stretching across Europe from the south-east; then followed the oak, which had appeared along the central zone of Europe before the close of the Magdalenian period, though pine forests still occupied northern latitudes.

The end of the Magdalenian period was accompanied by another slight elevation of the land, and consequent increase of cold; we seem here to have the third phase of the triple Bühl advance of the glaciers. The rise of the land cut off what is now the Baltic Sea, already free from ice, from the Arctic Ocean on the one hand and the North Sea on the other, thus converting it into a large lake or inland sea. This, from a fresh-water mollusc found abundantly in its bed, is known as the Ancylus Lake or Sea. The elevation and consequent cold period was not of long duration, and the land sank again, apparently to about fifty feet below its present level. This depression does not appear, however, for a time at least, to have opened the Ancylus Lake to the oceans. Meanwhile, the oak forest was spreading steadily northwards, and had reached Denmark, together with the Linden, Alder, and Hazel, before the close of the Ancylus period.

The closing in of the oak forest materially affected the life of the Magdalenian folk, who had gained their living by hunting the wild beasts of the steppe and afterwards the deer of the pine woods. Hunting in dense oak forests, often thick with undergrowth, was more difficult and dangerous, and the oncoming of the cool phase included under the name Bühl, with its accompaniment of increased rainfall in western Europe, had an adverse effect upon Magdalenian culture.

The changed conditions did not affect so acutely the Capsian people of East Spain. The climate here was drier, the forest advanced less rapidly, and when the last Magdalenian culture had come to an end, the Capsian civilization still continued in the phase known as 'Final Capsian' or 'Capso-Tardenoisian'. This industry is characterized by the presence of very small flints of geometric shapes, chiefly of trapezoid, rhomboid, and triangular forms ; these are commonly known as microliths. Speaking for the moment only of more southerly sites, we may say they are found also in North Africa and eastwards through Egypt, Syria, Mesopotamia, India, and Ceylon.

The wide extent of this southerly province of the microlithic industry suggests that about this time we have a new invasion

Palaeolithic Survivals 97

of Europe from North Africa, the people bearing with them some fresh elements of culture, though what these were is uncertain. We have seen that the storm zone, which had traversed the Mediterranean region during the Upper Palaeolithic period, had shifted to a more northerly course. During

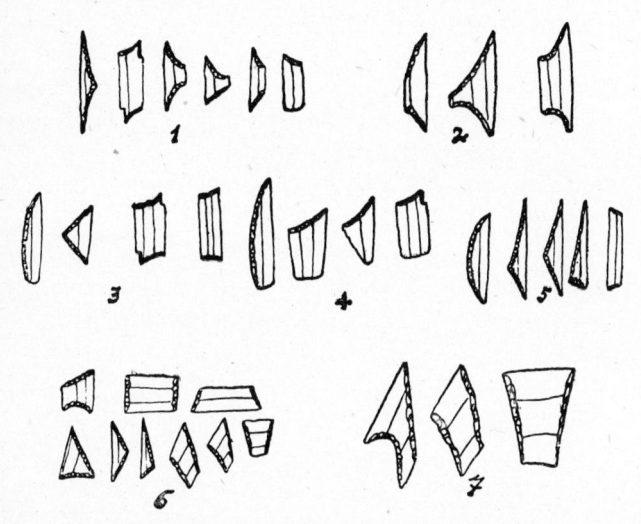

FIG. 53. Typical geometric flints. (After Breuil.)

the earlier time the Sahara region, lying only just to the south of the storm zone, must have received a moderate winter rainfall, and would have been a grassy steppe-land, where large numbers of men could have hunted an abundant supply of hoofed animals. What was true of the Sahara must also have been true of Arabia and Persia. With the northward drift of the storm zone the local rainfall diminished and nearly ceased; the steppe land, in consequence, passed to dry steppe and eventually to desert. The supply of game would thus have diminished, and the hunters, if they were to survive, must have followed them. It seems reasonable to suggest that a fairly uniform culture, of which the microlithic implements were a characteristic feature, had spread over the whole of this steppe region, and that, as it changed to desert, the hunters carried this culture to India and thence to Ceylon, into the valleys of the Jordan, the Euphrates, and the Nile, and perhaps southwards towards Nigeria.

Let us now turn to the spread of this culture in Europe under pressure of increasing drought in the Sahara. Bows and arrows were already well known in East Spain, and perhaps, too, to the later Magdalenians; but we may suspect that these new-comers were more expert bowmen, though the typical arrow-head had not yet been evolved. It seems likely that they had other advantages which enabled them to overcome their northern neighbours. Perhaps, however, it was merely a question of numbers.

The movement of their advance-guard seems to have been northwards into Cantabria, in northern Spain, where they amalgamated with such Magdalenians as were sheltering in the caves there, reduced to poverty by the inclement climate and the dearth of game. Here grew up a culture, showing elements both of Magdalenian and Final Capsian origin, which is known as Early Azilian, from the cave of Mas d'Azil, where it was first found.

This Early Azilian culture is characterized by a number of small round planing tools, many microliths, though rarely of geometric form, a few implements that remind us of Magdalenian tools and some flat harpoons. These harpoons deserve notice, for they differ considerably, both in form and material, from those used in the Magdalenian period. They are made of the horn of the red deer, instead of that of the reindeer, which by this time had retreated to the north. The change in the material caused the altered form, and it had become necessary to make them flat and not round.

The Early Azilian culture developed in due course into the

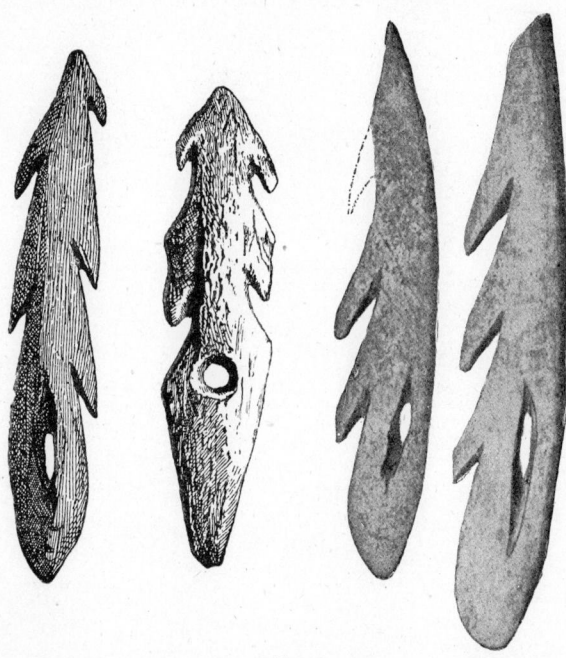

FIG. 54. Azilian harpoons.

Late Azilian, which is better known and more typical. This seems to have had a longer duration and is more widely distributed, and belongs to the time when the climate was again improving. It seems, in fact, especially in the north, to have lasted well into the milder parts of the Ancylus period, and, in Scotland at any rate, considerably later. In this phase the tools of Magdalenian type have disappeared, and many small microliths occur. The harpoons remain almost entirely unchanged, while we find a number of poor and badly made implements of bone. The most distinctive objects of this age are flat pebbles, with curious conventional designs painted upon them. Some writers have seen in these designs the germs of a system of writing, but Professor Obermaier considers them to be conventional treatment of the human and other forms, and suggests that they are idols.

The remains of these people, especially those found at Mas d'Azil, show that they fed largely on shell-fish, and that vegetable food formed an important item of their diet, for remains of acorns, haws, sloes, hazel-nuts, chestnuts, cherries, plums, and walnuts have been found there. A handful of barley seeds was also found, which has led to the suggestion that they cultivated grain ; this, however, was most probably gathered wild. The presence of harpoons shows that they added fish to their diet, and it is likely that some flesh food was added, if only occasionally. Still the Azilian folk were leading a lowly existence, usually by the shores of rivers, lakes, and the sea.

Remains of the Azilian period have been found fairly widely distributed, which shows us that, at any rate rather late in the period, these folk wandered far. Azilian sites have been found in many places in the north of Spain and the south of France. They stretched in the west as far as the British Isles, for remains of this culture have been found in a cave at Settle in Yorkshire, at Whitburn in Durham, near Kirkcudbright, in two caves near Oban, and on five sites in the island of Oronsay. A deposit found in a cave at Ofnet in Bavaria belongs to this period, but it is by no means certain that the remains are of the same people. The tools do not very closely resemble

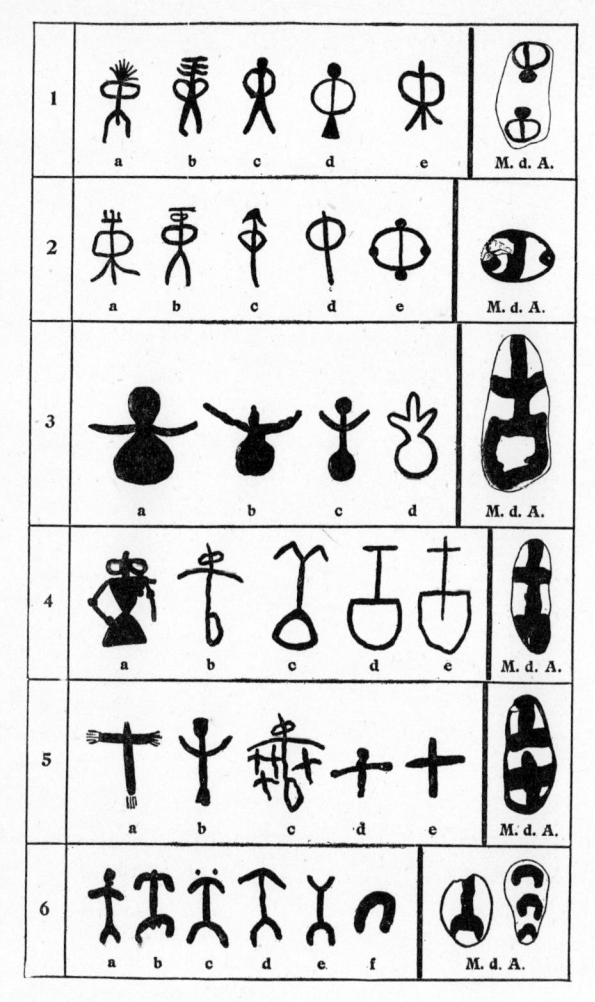

FIG. 55. Spanish petroglyphs, representing human figures more or less conventionalized, compared with similar designs from the painted pebbles of Mas d'Azil.

typical Azilian implements, but collars were found, made of stags' teeth, which closely resemble some found at Mas d'Azil. Typical Azilian harpoons and painted pebbles have, however, been found near Basle in Switzerland.

Contemporary with the Late Azilian deposits are some found at Mugem, on the banks of the Tagus not far from Lisbon. Here we have another riverside settlement. The remains consist of a number of shell-mounds, situated about forty miles from the mouth of the river and from twenty to twenty-five metres above the present sea-level. This suggests that the coast-line was then about fifty feet above its present level, which is what we believe it to have been in the Baltic at the middle of the Ancylus period. The implements are mainly geometric flints, resembling the Final Capsian type, and a few simple bone tools. The remains of their meals show us that they fed on wild cattle, sheep or goat, horse, swine, dog or wolf, and several other smaller animals, though their diet consisted mainly of shell-fish. It is clear that they neither cultivated grain nor kept domesticated animals, except perhaps the dog. Some potsherds, found in the upper layers of the mounds, are believed to date from a much later period. The resemblance of the microlithic flints to implements of the Final Capsian culture suggests that this is another instance of the distribution of these latest of the Capsian invaders.

The main advance, however, of the Final Capsian hunters was rather to the east of north. Starting, apparently, somewhat later than those who went to Cantabria, they pushed round the eastern flank of the Pyrenees and to the west of the Central Plateau of France, whence they proceeded in the direction of the Baltic Sea, in an endeavour, it would seem, to get beyond the zone of the oak forest. On their way across southern France they appear to have met with some of the

Palaeolithic Survivals 103

advance-guard who had already evolved the Early Azilian culture, for they seem to have added some elements from this civilization to their own. Farther north, as we shall see, they came into contact with still another culture.

From the town of Fère-en-Tardenois, in the neighbourhood of which this culture was first noticed, it is called Tardenoisian

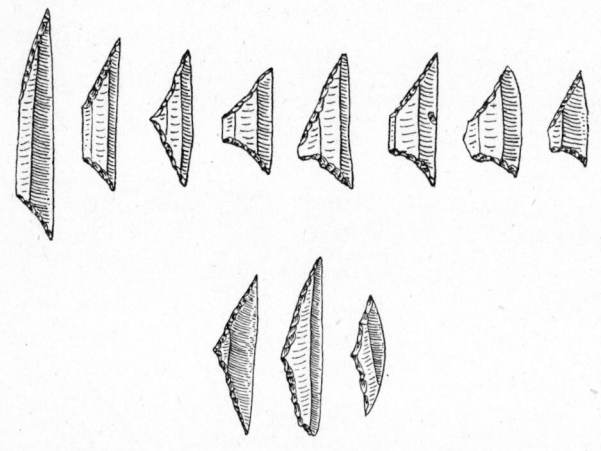

FIG. 56. Geometric flints from Mugem. (After Breuil.)

and we may distinguish two main phases of it, called Early and Late Tardenoisian. This industry consists mainly of the use of microlithic flint implements of geometric form, with a few elements derived from the Late Azilian culture. It has not, as yet, received as close a study as it deserves, and the fact that it is not usually found in caves but in the open has made the discovery of habitation sites difficult. It is not yet easy to define the difference between the early and late flint types, though the latter seem to be smaller, or at least narrower, than the former.

This industry seems to have spread widely along a zone of

country in Europe on which the soil was not of a character to encourage dense forest growth. This is a zone which we shall often have occasion to mention in later parts of this series. Its loose, friable, dry soil, where it occurs in central and eastern Europe, is called loess. In northern France it is of different character, and is called Plateau Alluvium.

The zone, broadly considered, stretches in patches from northern France eastwards beyond South Germany and Bohemia to the lower lands both south and north of the Carpathians and on to South Russia to meet the Asiatic Steppe. Along our zone Tardenoisian culture slowly spread to Poland, Crimea, and the Kirghiz Steppe. It also ultimately spread in the west, and has been identified as far north as the Yorkshire moors and East Scotland, as well as at a number of spots on the west coasts of England and Wales. It is possible that the Ofnet deposits should be considered as belonging to this culture, in spite of the presence of the stags' tooth necklaces.

The art of this period is very different from that which preceded it. The conventionalization, which had been in progress in late Magdalenian times, had reached its acme, and we find only apparently meaningless designs, which may, perhaps, stand for human figures; we see also some drawings, which are called 'tectiform', and which may represent huts or tents. There is so much general resemblance, in spite of local differences, between the various cultures of this period, that they are usually all included in the term Azilio-Tardenoisian. Though the definitely Azilian features occur more in the west and near the coast, and the more typical Tardenoisian in the east and inland, we must be careful not to assume too great a distinction between them, or to fail to make allowance for the many interchanges of ideas and products which seem to have taken place.

Early in the Ancylus period, before the aspen had given place to the fir, we first meet with certain evidence of human settlement in the Baltic region. This is the Nörre-Lyngby culture of Denmark, Scania, Rügen, and Northern Prussia. The characteristic features of this culture are coarsely flaked spear-heads with tangs and reindeer-horn axes; some harpoons of reindeer horn, which seem to be degenerate descendants of

Fig. 57. Tent-shaped designs. (After Capitan, Breuil, and Peyrony.)

Magdalenian models, may also belong to this culture. The close resemblance between these spear-heads and some found in the bed of the Bann in the north of Ireland, which, however, are somewhat later in date, leads us to suspect a western extension also.

Recently, Kozłowski has described a culture which he has found at Chwalibogowice, a village situated at the eastern end of the Polish sand dune area, at a point on the Vistula about fifty miles below Cracow. Certain large arrow-heads or spear-heads found here seem to resemble those of Nörre-Lyngby, and as they were found several feet below a deposit containing implements of Tardenoisian type, we must consider them as earlier rather than later than the Danish specimens. Kosłowski has lately recognized implements as belonging to this culture among some found by Leslie Armstrong in Holderness. If these views be accepted, this culture arose in the loess or steppe regions, and spread thence to the shores of the Baltic, while it extended later to the Yorkshire coast and even to the north of Ireland.

During the latter part of the Ancylus period we find cultures, perhaps slightly connected with that of Nörre-Lyngby and in the same region; these are the industries found at Maglemose, near Mullerup, and at Svaerdborg, both in Denmark. It is customary to speak of these as the Maglemose civilization. In these the flint implements are very like the Tardenoisian in form, and the generally held view is that this culture represents the farthest extension to the north of the Final Capsian invasion. On the other hand, there are marked differences, such as the greater use of bone implements, sometimes of a finer type and including new forms, and the more naturalistic style of the engravings. These features are thought by some to be due to influences from a Magdalenian culture which survived late in Poland, and it must not be forgotten that the Abbé Breuil has compared these engravings with some discovered in Siberia. The problem is not yet solved, but we must conclude that the Maglemose culture is the product of the mixture of Tardenoisian with perhaps more than one other element. Maglemose bone harpoons have been found in Northern France and Belgium, and some of these have Tardenoisian triangular flints fixed to serve as barbs. We also note that an Upper Palaeolithic site with harpoons has been discovered at Wercholensk near Irkutsk, in Siberia.

The Maglemose culture has been found along the south of the Baltic from Hanover to East Prussia, and, according to

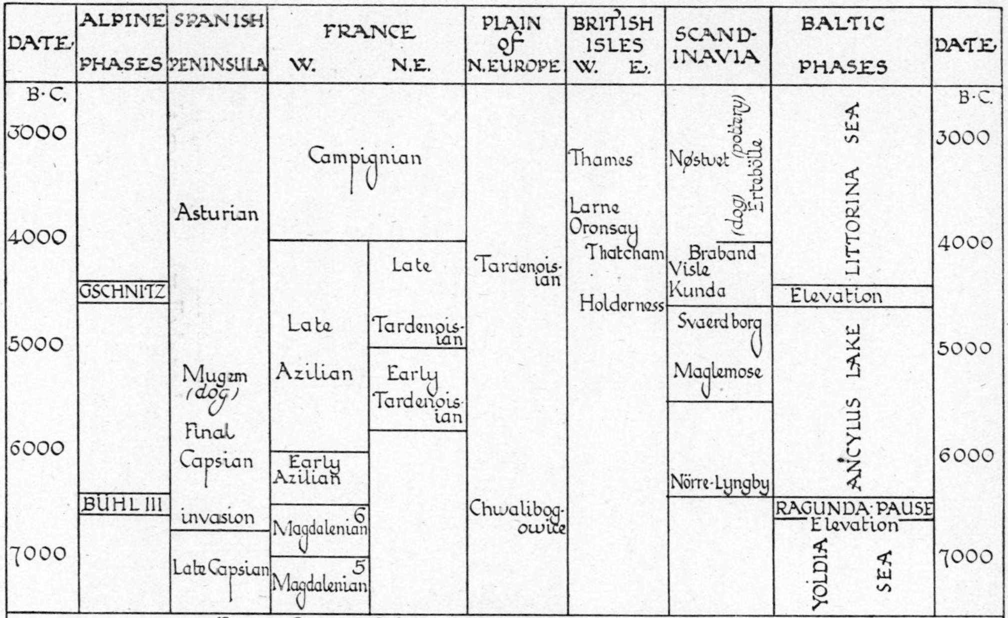

Fig. 58. Chart of the Mesolithic or Epipalaeolithic Period.

Note. The chart reads, in order of time, from the bottom upwards.

Obermaier, farther east still at Kunda in Estonia, though this site is usually considered to date from the succeeding period. What appears to be a late phase of it occurs also in the Holderness region of Yorkshire, while the Azilian deposits in Scotland show Maglemose affinities. The people seem to have lived upon rafts or platforms, made of tree trunks, in the shallow waters of lakes or bays of the inland Ancylus Sea.

During the closing phase of the Ancylus period the land again rose, so that the coast-line was about fifteen fathoms below its present level, and the southern part of the North Sea became dry land. This it was which enabled the Maglemose people to migrate as far west as Holderness. This elevation of the land by ninety feet must have caused a perceptible increase in the severity of the climate, especially in the neighbourhood of mountains, and we would link this with the Gschnitz stage in the Alps. After this the land sank again to about twenty-five feet below its present level, and the climate improved considerably. The sea broke through the Danish islands into the Baltic, converting it into a very saline sea, twice as salt as at present; from the prevailing mollusc found in its bed, this sea is called the Littorina Sea. The climate was milder even than to-day, for this is the time known as the 'climatic optimum', and towards its close the beech tree first appeared in Denmark.

This period, known as the Littorina period, is the time of the 'kitchen middens' or shell-mounds, when the people of the Baltic lived chiefly by the sea-shore, feeding on shell-fish, and casting away the shells, which formed huge mounds upon the beach. Two phases of this culture are usually recognized. The first may be called the Brabrand phase, after the lake of that name in East Jutland, and it includes such sites as that at Viste, which shows, perhaps, a rather earlier stage. The second

Palaeolithic Survivals

or chief phase, which seems to have been of considerable duration, is called the Ertebölle phase, after the well-known shell-mound at that place in Jutland. The first phase has some-

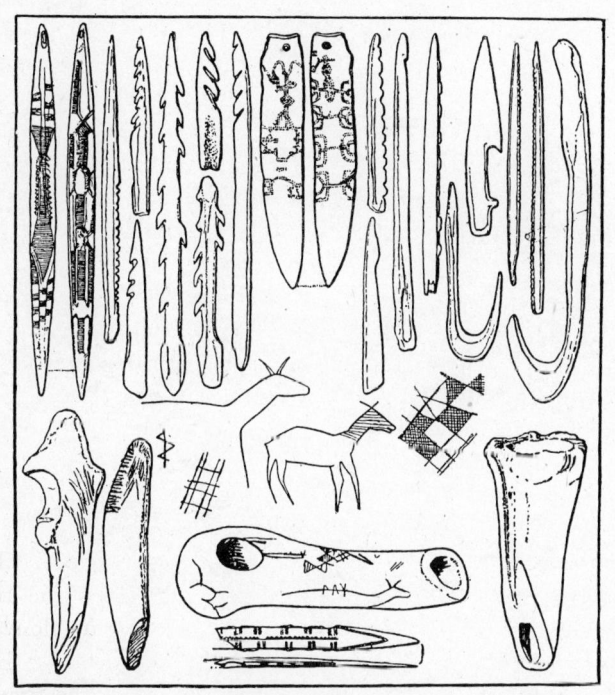

FIG. 59. The Maglemose industry. (After P. Reinecke.)

times been named from Kunda, a culture site in Estonia, but since Obermaier has recently claimed this as a late site of the Maglemose culture, the name is best abandoned.

As distinguished from the Maglemose culture, where bone implements were commoner than tools of flint, in the shell-mounds flint implements predominate. At this stage we begin to find axes so chipped as to have the cutting edge at right angles to the length of the implement. The butt is always pointed, so the axe is typically triangular. Harpoons, reminiscent of the Maglemose period, occur, though rarely, during the first period, especially at Kunda, but during the second phase bone tools include only scoops, needles, bodkins, and towards the end, combs. Coarse pottery, always in fragments, has been found during the second phase, and probably belongs to the close of the period; whether the art was introduced from elsewhere, and if so from what region, or whether it was an independent discovery, will be discussed in a later part; it seems to be the first evidence of the potter's art in western or northern Europe. The people were still in a hunting or collecting stage, living on shell-fish, birds, fish, and more rarely mammals, but there seems to be no doubt that they possessed domesticated dogs, and it has been suggested that they must have had boats, as the bones of deep-sea fish have been found among their refuse.

No shell-mounds exactly comparable with those of Scandinavia have been found outside the Baltic area, but in the Kennet valley in England a somewhat similar site has been explored. This was situated on a gravel bank, almost if not entirely surrounded by water, especially in flood time, on what is now the sewage station of the borough of Newbury. This site, known as the Thatcham site, from the parish in which it is situated, produced a small number of roughly flaked axes, with pointed butts and the transverse cutting edge, and a larger number of small finely worked implements, in some respects resembling those from Svaerdborg. Though the Thatcham industry by no means completely resembles that of the shell-mounds, it seems to be not wholly unconnected with it, and is probably contemporary rather with Brabrand than with

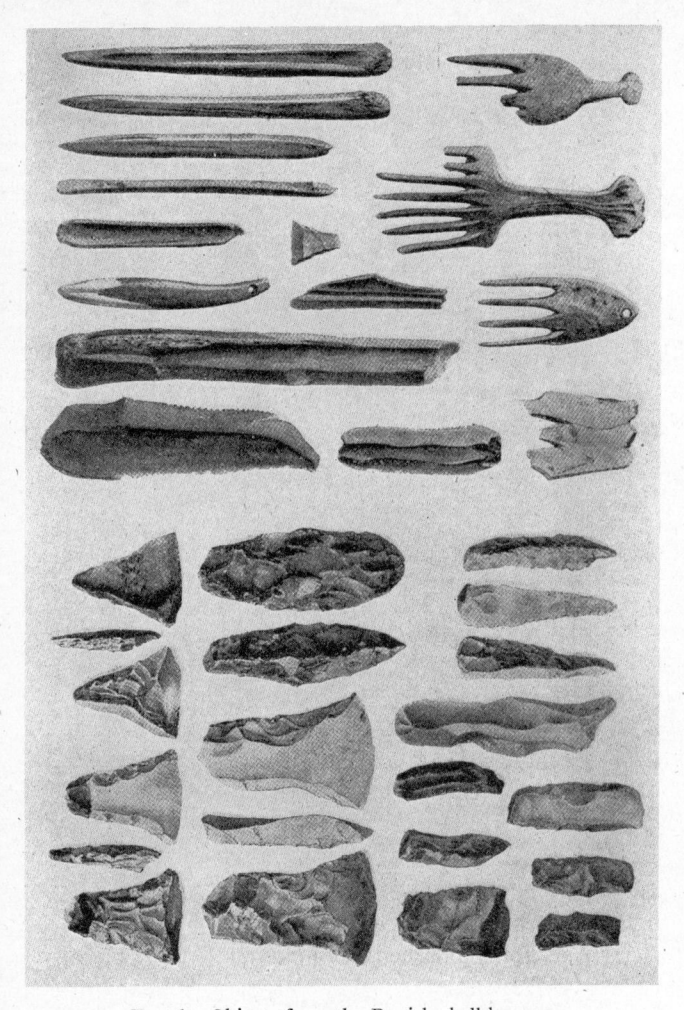

FIG. 60. Objects from the Danish shell-heaps.

Ertbölle. It dates, in all probability, from the very beginning of the Littorina period, before the land had sunk sufficiently to bar the way between Denmark and the east of England.

At Nøstvet, in the south of Norway, has been found a culture very similar to that of the shell-mounds, dating from the time of the maximum of the Littorina depression. Here have been

FIG. 61. Pottery from the shell-heaps.

found certain axes or picks, made from crystalline rock, very similar to the picks, from the hill of Le Campigny, near the town of Blangy-sur-Bresle, Seine Inférieure, where a site was explored in 1872. This site has given the name to a period, and the name has sometimes been applied widely to include the culture of Nøstvet and the whole shell-mound civilization. It is now thought, however, that the type station of Le Campigny dates from a much later time, from the dawn of the Metal Age, for a polished axe was found there; also it has been noticed that the type of pick in question, while it occurs in some of the earlier shell-mounds, lasts right on to the Metal Age; it has even been found in Early Iron Age deposits,

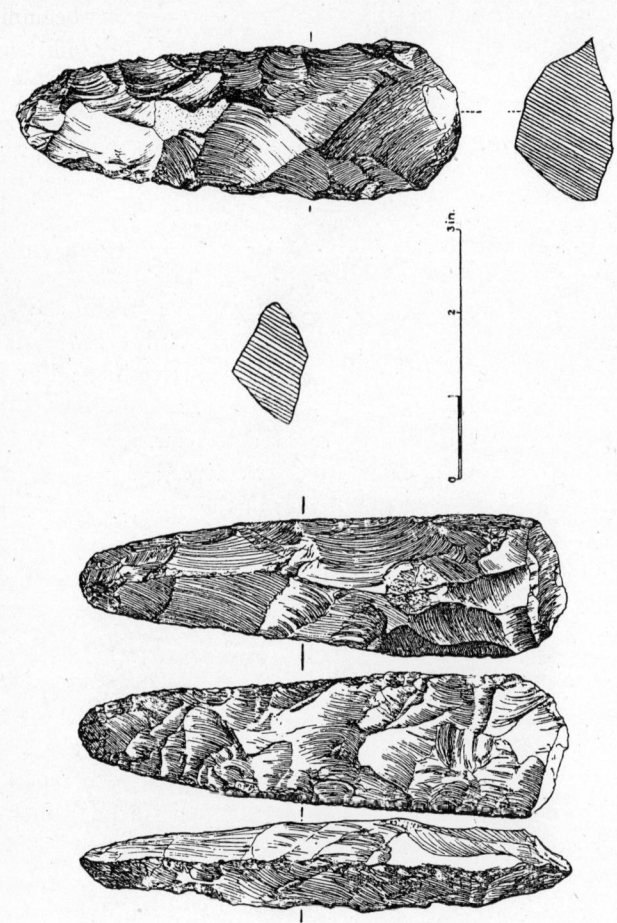

FIG. 62. Flint axes from Thatcham.

including one in Casterley camp, Wilts., recently reported by Mrs. Cunnington, and another found at Grimes Graves by Leslie Armstrong, associated with Early Iron Age pottery.

Campignian picks have been found in most parts of Europe except the extreme south, but we cannot be sure that all these belong to the shell-mound period. Two sites in England seem, however, to date from this time, those of the Cissbury pits and Grimes Graves. Both these sites, where flint was mined, were occupied for a very lengthy period, and it seems probable that both lasted on almost if not quite to the Metal Age. At Larne, in the north of Ireland, on a raised beach dating, apparently, from the middle of the Littorina period, a number of such picks have been found, and in the Bann a particular type of large arrow-head or spear-head, which seems, as we have seen, to be derived from the Nörre-Lyngby culture; other such sites have been found in the north-west of the island.

It has been suggested that this Campignian pick is a new element in the culture of Europe, which must have been introduced by a new people, and various suggestions have been made to account for its appearance. Kozłowski has quite recently suggested that the Campignian industry came from Syria across South Russia to Poland and across North Russia to Scandinavia, and that later it spread from Poland to the West of Europe. The evidence at present available seems scarcely sufficient to support so far-reaching an hypothesis. It seems to us that there is more to be said for the alternative hypothesis that the new implements were called into being by a new demand. We have seen that, owing to the spread of the oak forest, most men were living by the shores of the sea or on the banks of lakes and rivers, leading a precarious existence and feeding on fish, shell-fish, nuts and berries, with very occasional meals of flesh-food. On the chalk downs of south-eastern England

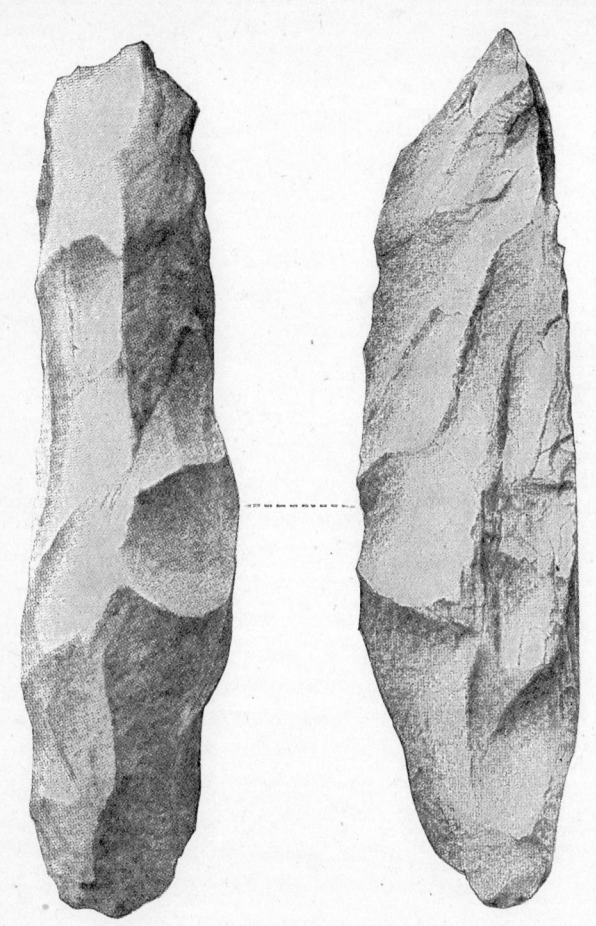

FIG. 63. Nøstvet axes. (After Brøgger.)

and the sandy lands of Norfolk the oak forest had little chance, owing to the dry nature of the subsoil, and the same was true of many loess areas on the Continent. In avoiding the woodland many men came and occupied these clear spaces, and found no fish or molluscs. Flesh-food being hard to come by, some may have added to their food supply by digging up edible roots. For this purpose these Campignian picks, mounted as hoes, would have been most suitable tools.

In Aurignacian times, though implements were usually made of flakes, core tools were not unknown. The Magdalenian inhabitants of south-western France did not use such implements, for the art of working large blocks of flint had fallen into disuse during their sojourn in the north of Spain when fleeing from the Solutrean invasion. But core implements continued to be used by the descendants of the Aurignacians in Magdalenian times elsewhere in Europe. Core implements formed no part of the stock-in-trade of the Final Capsian invaders, for they are not found in Tardenoisian deposits, and only rarely at Maglemose. Their reappearance in the shell-mound period seems to betoken a fusion in north Europe between the last Capsian invaders and the descendants of the northern Aurignacians, who found a new use for these core implements in digging up edible roots; some change of form, of course, took place to meet the needs of the new occupation. This may perhaps explain the fact, which has puzzled some archaeologists, that some of the implements from Grimes Graves have a strangely Aurignacian appearance.

Away from the sea-coast on the continent of Europe it is possible that a late phase of the Tardenoisian culture may still have lingered, for it is believed by some to have come into contact with fully developed Neolithic civilization. It may be that this survival co-existed there with Campignian picks.

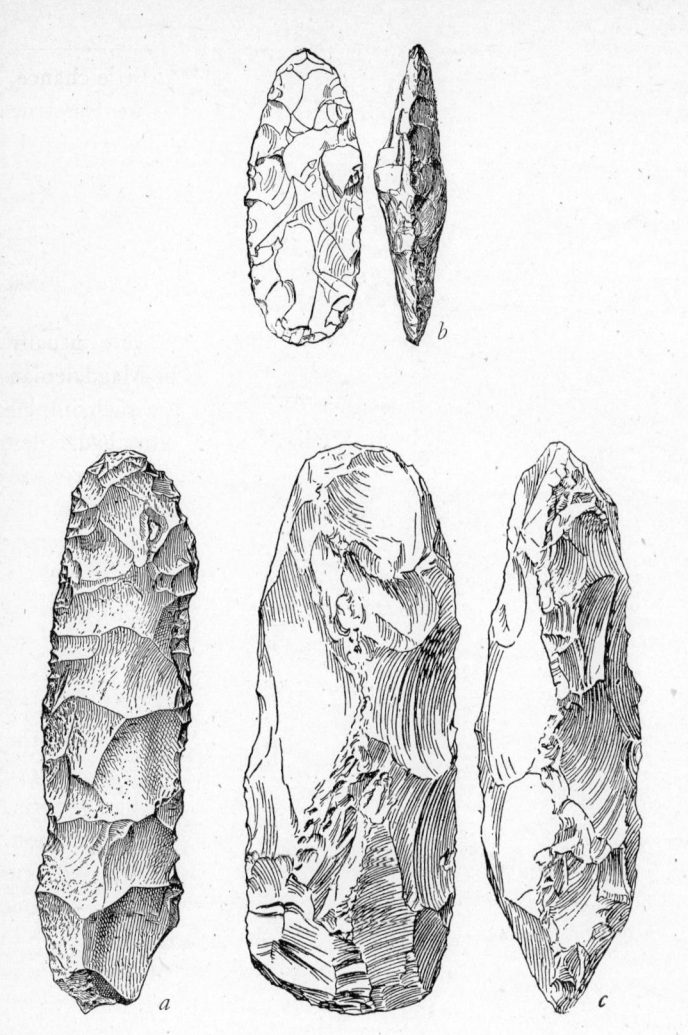

FIG. 64. Picks from (*a*) Campigny, (*b*) Cissbury, and (*c*) Grimes Graves.

One apparently new culture appears in western Europe during the shell-mound period, in the province of Asturias in the north of Spain. This, too, is a true shell-mound culture,

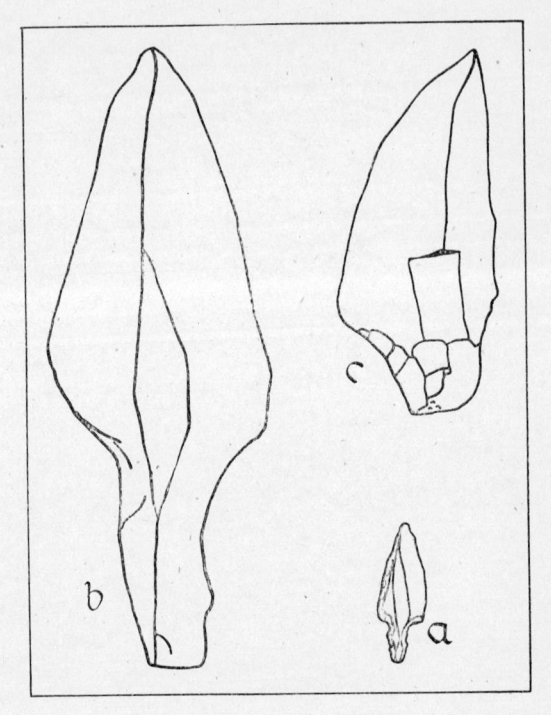

FIG. 65. Spear-heads from (*a*) Chwalibogowice, (*b*) Nörre-Lyngby, and (*c*) Bann.

found always on the sea-coast, but besides the shells of cockles, limpets, and top-shells, remains are found of stag, roe deer, horse, cattle, wild boar, and many other smaller animals. The only implements so far found are some roughly flaked tools made from pebbles, which have quite a Lower Palaeolithic appearance. The only implements of other material which

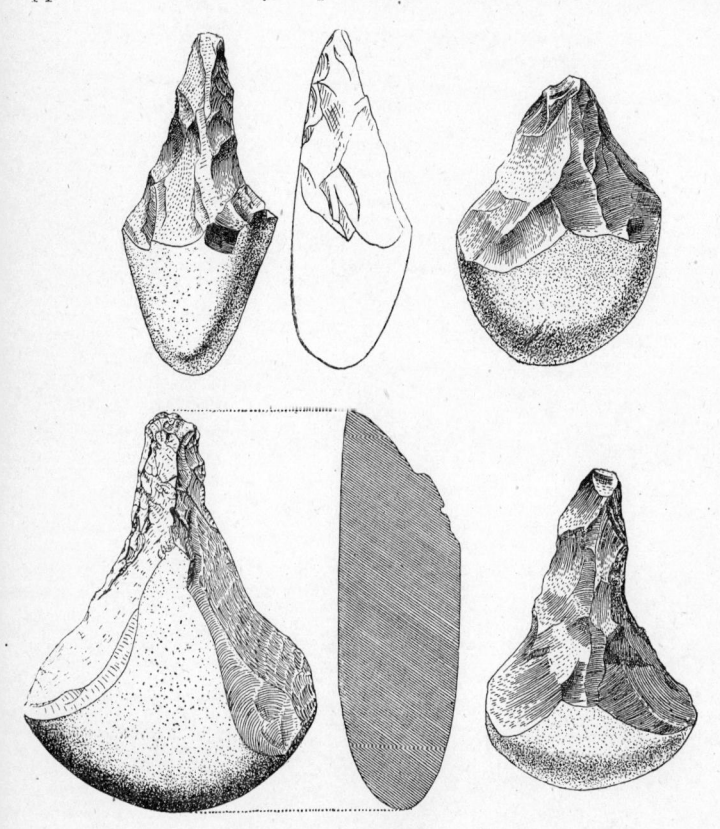

FIG. 66. Stone implements of Asturian type.

have been discovered are two tools, of unknown use, made of the side antlers of a stag, each perforated with a hole. A few implements of this industry have been found on the adjoining coast of France, but so far little is known of this Asturian industry. It has been found also at Islandmagee, Ireland.

The industries dealt with in this chapter are best classed together as Mesolithic, though some writers prefer the term Epipalaeolithic. They appear to have lasted for several thousands of years, and to have come down to fairly recent times, that is to a period long after the beginnings of true civilization had appeared in the East. From his former hunting activities with the accompanying virile art, man had been debarred by the oncoming oak forest: he had sunk to the level of a mere collector of food, a feeder on roots, nuts, berries, and shellfish, varied by a small amount of fish and flesh food. The only advances made during this time had been the introduction of the domesticated dog, and towards its close in Denmark the use of rough pottery. The people might have continued indefinitely in a state resembling the present inhabitants of Tierra del Fuego, had not fresh elements of culture reached them from the south-east.

BOOKS

MACALISTER, R. A. S. *A Text-book of European Archaeology*, vol. i (1921).
OBERMAIER, H. *Fossil Man in Spain* (1924).
SOLLAS, W. J. *Ancient Hunters* (1924).
CHILDE, V. GORDON. *The Dawn of European Civilization* (1925).

8

Late Palaeolithic Invaders of Europe

A COMPARISON of the list at the end of this chapter with that which appeared at the end of chapter 5 at once demonstrates that there is a marked contrast between these people and nearly all their predecessors, except the people of Solutré. Whereas in Aurignacian, Solutrean, and Magdalenian times the people seem to have been nearly all long-headed, with the exception of the Solutré specimens, those of the later group include a long-headed group, which carries on the characters, especially of the Predmost–Combe Capelle stock, but there is also an important broad-headed element contrasting strikingly with the first. At Ofnet, Mugem, and Aveline's Hole the two elements occur side by side, showing intermingling of the two stocks, as most students think, for the contrasts are usually quite marked. The associations are clearly with Tardenoisian implements in all three cases. Ochre was used in the burials at Ofnet as it was in the earlier burials at Brünn. Ornaments of bored shells decorated the children and most of the women at Ofnet, and the two young men had them too. The women had collars or belts of deers' teeth, and some of the children also had a few. The two elder men had neither type of ornament, but they and some of the women, and even a few of the children, had flint implements.

The Ofnet skulls were in two groups, Group I with 27, and Group II with 6. They represent a succession of burials, all facing the sunset; the earlier burials in the course of time became thronged at the centre. The youth of the individuals is noteworthy: 12 or 13 were infants, 6 were children, 10 were women, and 4 were men ; but none of the men seem to have been over 40 and none of the women much above 30 years of age. One cannot but infer that the average duration of life, even apart from numerous deaths in infancy, was low, and this inference is more or less confirmed by the study of burials elsewhere. The use of ochre, bored snail shells, and flints as grave furniture, suggests inheritances from earlier European cultures, but the grouping and orientation of the skulls may be a new feature. Obermaier has drawn attention to the similarity between these groupings of skulls and the groupings in the skull altars described by F. Sarasin in New Caledonia. There the skulls are held in high honour, and the people come to them to beseech the spirits of their forefathers for help. If the arrangement at Ofnet is really like that in New Caledonia, we have here indications of the veneration of the dead ; the idea of an ' All Souls ' festival may be of immense antiquity. The development of such an idea would mark an upward step in man's mental development, the origination of a fairly conscious social tradition. It is tempting, but not justifiable as yet, to argue that the long-headed individuals at Ofnet are related to the earlier European elements in the culture, and that the broad-headed skulls are related to the newer elements.

We have seen in an earlier chapter that Aurignacian men show a marked increase in the length of the head as compared with most Mousterian men, though we must not suppose the former to be descendants of the latter. The ancestors of Aurignacian men may well have been less long-headed than these. They may have had the brow ridges strong in some cases and almost absent in others, but probably the ridges above the two brows did not fuse into a great frontal torus like that of the Mousterian men. It may also have happened that some of those ancestors developed in other ways and

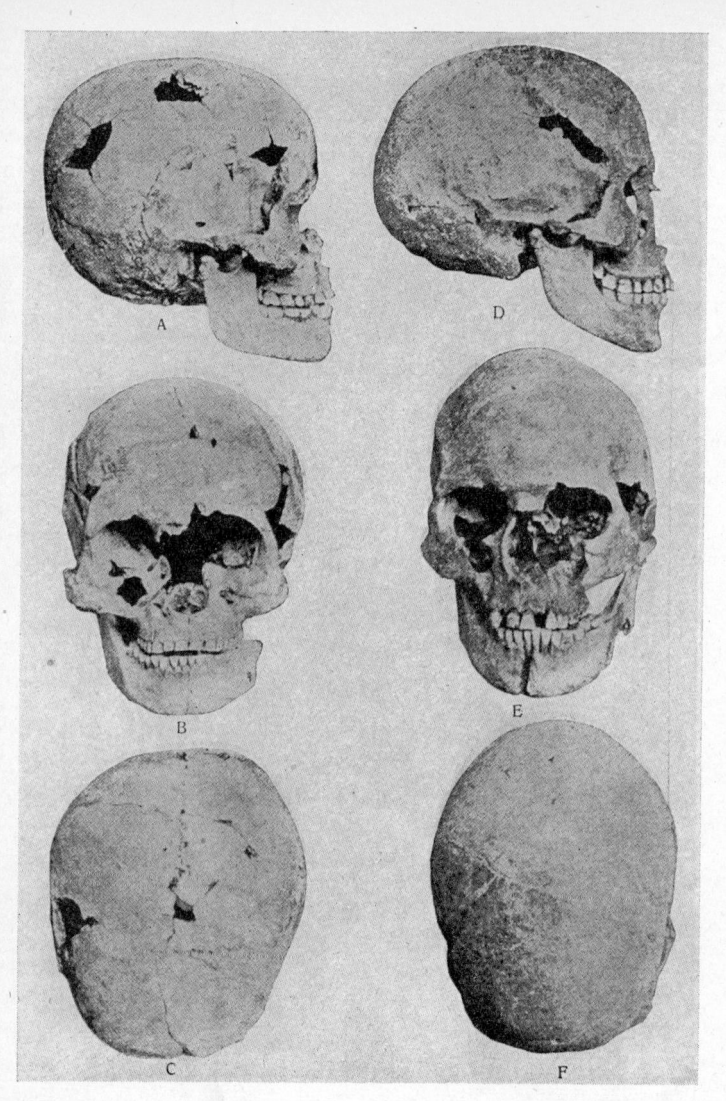

FIG. 67. Skulls from the cave of Ofnet, Bavaria. (After F. Birkner.)

became broader-headed instead of longer-headed. Suggestions have been made that a habit of using the teeth to tear flesh would so strengthen the temporal muscles as to keep the skull narrow, and thus, if it grew, it would grow in length. On the other hand, patient mastication with the molar teeth

FIG. 68. Altar of skulls in New Caledonia. (After F. Sarasin.)

would not do this to anything like the same extent, and a diet of small stuff, collected rather than hunted, would be eaten in this way.

If modern men are all the descendants of one palaeolithic type, and this is by no means proved, even if we believe in the unity of the origin of man, that type had a head neither very long nor very broad. It would certainly be a mistake to suppose that the longest-headed types of modern man, *Homo sapiens*, are necessarily the oldest and that evolution has proceeded from the longest to the broadest type. Far more probably a moderately long head represents the early type, if there is *one* such type, and the very long heads and the broad

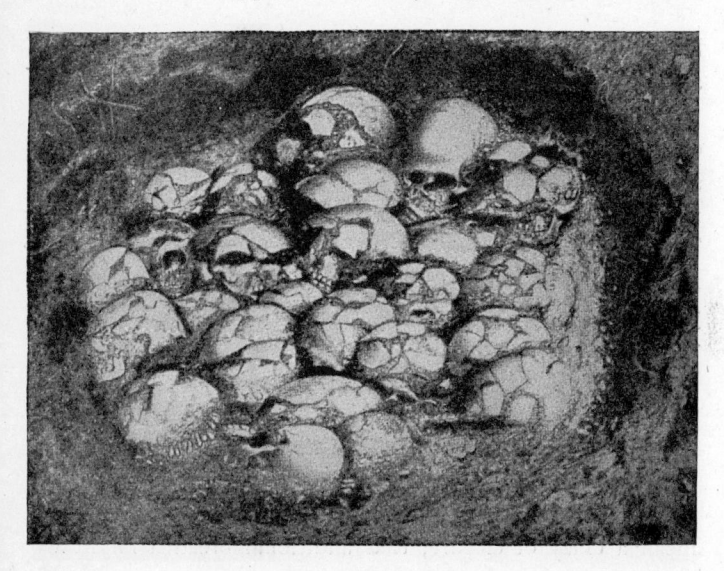

FIG. 69. Group of skulls at Ofnet. (After R. R. Schmidt.)

heads represent divergent lines of evolution from it. However that may be, the distribution of broad-headedness in modern populations suggests that this character had one centre of origin, possibly in Anatolia. Its present distribution in western Europe is especially in the Alpine region, in the broad sense of the term. Ofnet, Furfooz, and Solutré may be said to lie round about the fringe of the Alpine region. Is it thus possible that in the ancient burials at these places we have remains of individuals who represent an early wave of a spread from the east? Further, may they have extended into the Alpine region as its valleys became clear of the superabundant water which must have lain in many boulder-clay hollows for ages after the great ice-sheets waned? If there be anything in these speculations, one might expect the broad-headed people of these ancient burials to preserve stages in the evolution of broad-headedness, and it is tempting to think that this is the case.

Nos. 3, 4, 5, 7, 8, 9, 10, and 11 of Catalogue A at the end of this chapter all show a double curve in the outline of the skull, as seen from above. The frontal region shows one curve markedly discontinuous with the curve of the posterior region. This suggests a broadening of the back of the skull, while the front for a time remained narrow. As is well known, the front part of the median or sagittal suture of the skull closes and vanishes at an early stage of our growth, save in a few individuals. This gives a firmness to the cover of that part of the brain which is associated with the higher qualities of intellect; it also gives strength to the framework supporting the eyes and teeth, and a firm basis for a part of the jaw muscles. We can well understand that, as additional breadth here would mean a delay of closure, that additional breadth might well have its coming delayed; indeed, in nearly all normal broad heads the point of maximum width is far back. All that can be hinted for the present is that the 'double-curve' Ofnet skulls may thus show us a stage in the evolution of broad-headedness.

It is noteworthy that these broad-heads rarely have the brow ridges strong, and the forward projection of the mouth is less than in earlier types. No. 22 of Catalogue A, however, has the brow ridges very strong, and at least two of the other Mugem skulls, one a long head, show projecting mouths.

There seems, by the way, little reason to suppose that broad-headedness spread into Europe by way of Spain and Portugal, so that region would be an ultimate corner of Europe for this

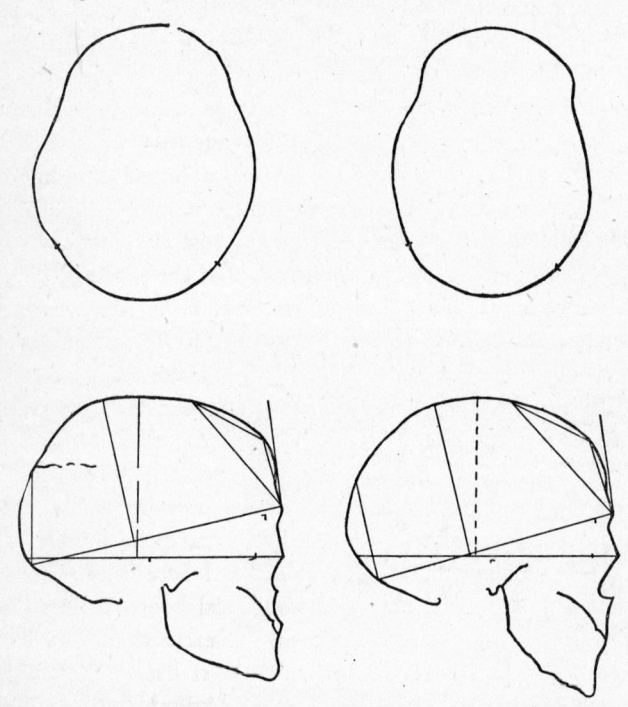

FIG. 70. *Norma verticalis* views of 'double-curved' skulls from Ofnet.

purpose, and we might expect to find old features persisting even alongside of the presumedly intrusive broad-headedness.

It seems fair to suggest that the long-heads in Catalogue A come nearer in skull form to the stocks represented by the Brünn, the Combe Capelle, and the still undescribed Predmost skulls than to the Cro-Magnon stock. No. 1 of Catalogue A has the head very high, height more than 100 per cent. of breadth and 71·5 per cent. of length, and it also has a relatively broad nose. No. 2 of Catalogue A again has the head high, though here the nose is narrower and the face shorter. No. 23 of Catalogue A has the head very high indeed and a projecting mouth.

Turning to the British Isles it seems reasonably clear that

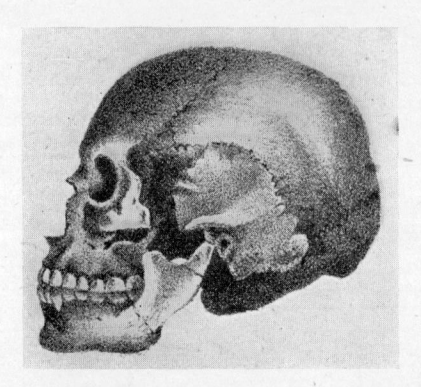

FIG. 71. Profile of a prognathous skull from Mugem.

the Cheddar, No. 1, Aveline's Hole, No. 13, and MacArthur Cave, No. 41, skulls date from the end of the Palaeolithic Age or later. They are specimens in which the head is high, and there are other resemblances to the Predmost–Combe Capelle group. The so-called river-bed skulls, typified by No. 2 of Catalogue B, also have the high head; this is especially true for the Tilbury, Halling, and Langwith skulls, while No. 8 of the same catalogue shows the relative height as very great indeed. It is interesting to note that Catalogue B includes so few broad skulls, especially as the paucity of broad-heads in the British population is still a feature.

Late Palaeolithic Invaders of Europe

We are inclined to suggest that the Aurignacian, Solutrean, and Magdalenian inhabitants of western Europe survived on through the end of the Palaeolithic Age, and that among them the heritage of the Combe Capelle–Predmost type of head spread widely. Possibly it was accompanied by some facial characters such as the narrower nose and the shorter, broader face derived

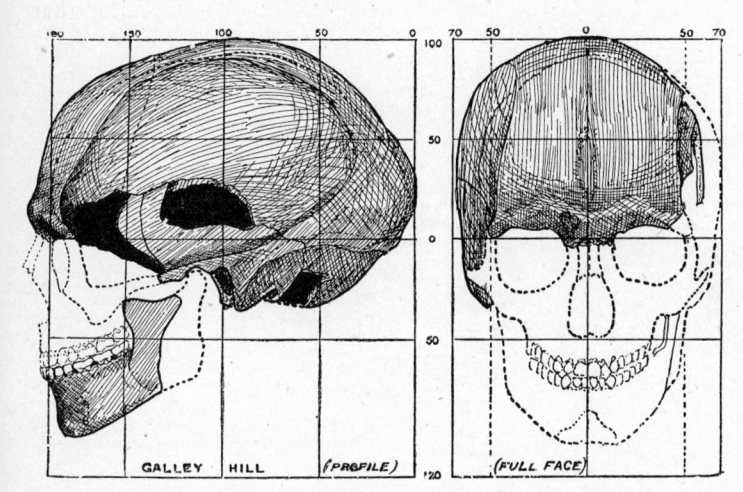

FIG. 72. Side and front view of the Galley Hill skull.

from the Cro-Magnon stock, or perhaps in both we have indications of effects on nose and chin of sharpening of the profile and jaw reduction. Stature does not seem to have run high in most cases, the absence of the tall strain noted on the Riviera and at Cro-Magnon for an earlier period being very noticeable.

Into this population there would seem to have drifted extraneous elements with more or less broadened heads, first found, if the local workers' dates be accepted, at Solutré, but

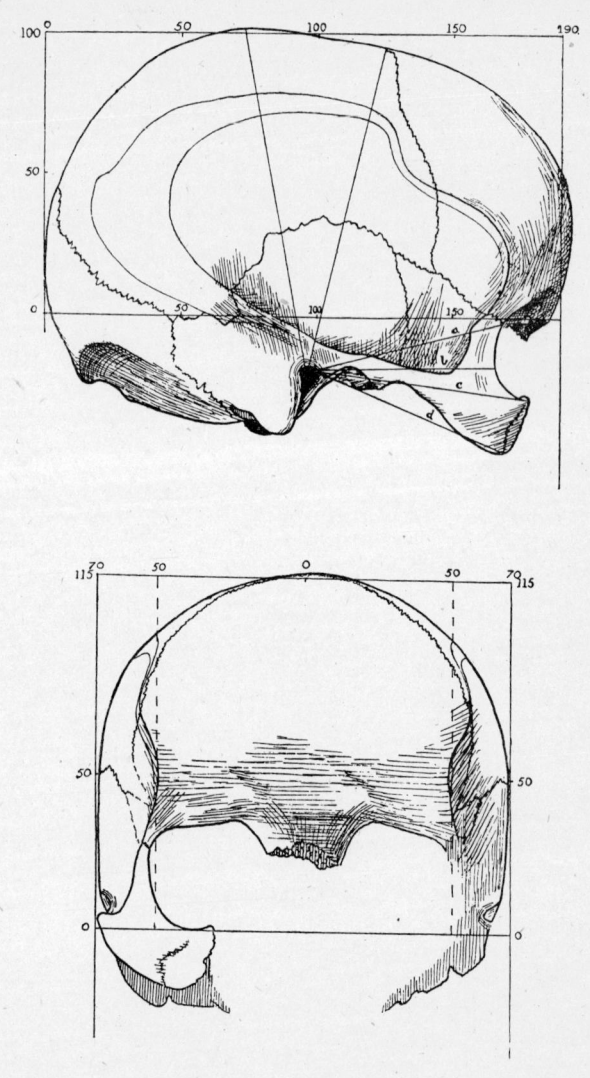

FIG. 73. Side and front view of skull from Aveline's Hole.

afterwards forming a marked feature at Ofnet, where we meet with what seem new funeral rites, new at all events for western Europe, unless the lost Aurignac collection of skulls was something of this kind. These extraneous elements may well have spread from the east along the foot-hills of the mountain ranges, and especially along the Galician Silesian-Moravian-Bavarian loess zone, their paucity in Britain at least does not militate against this view. Finally, among these extraneous elements we seem to get hints of stages in the evolution of broad-headedness.

APPENDIX

A. SKULLS AND SKELETONS OF THE END OF THE PALAEOLITHIC AGE, INCLUDING SOME OF RATHER DOUBTFUL DATE.

1. Ofnet 21. 1. Man, 25 years of age. L. 200, B. 141, H. 143, C.I. 70·5, Bz. 132 ?, Orbit 29/41, Nose 26/42, C.C. 1500. Brow ridges strong, cheek-bones fairly strong, mouth does not project forwards, chin strong, face rather short and broad.
2. Ofnet 24. 1. Man, 30-40 years. L. 190, B. 140, C.I. 73·7, H. 137, Bz. 132, Orbit 34/40, Nose 24/52, C.C. 1420. Brow ridges weak, face broad and short, chin weak.
3. Ofnet 2. 1. Man, 30-40 years. L. 182, B. 146, C.I. 80·2 (78·6), H. 118, Bz. 141, Orbit 30/34, Nose 21/51. Brow ridges weak, face broad and short, chin weak.
4. Ofnet 11. 1. Man, 22 years. L. 183, B. 144, C.I. 78·7, H. 135, Bz. 140, Orbit ?, Nose 24/49. Brow ridges practically absent.

The two last skulls, when looked at from above, have an outline which seems to be made up of very different curves, one in front and the other at the back. For brevity, this character, when mentioned below, will be designated simply 'double curve'.

5. Ofnet 3. 1. Woman, 20 years. L. 162, B. 144, C.I. 88·9, H. 129, Bz. 142, Orbit 28/35, Nose 19/41. Mouth projects forward, double curve.

6. Ofnet 4. 1. Woman, 30 years. L. 175, B. 150, C.I. 86·2, H. 142, Bz. 128, Orbit 28/35, Nose ?/49, C.C. 1400. Markedly high, because of the great height of the head.
7. Ofnet 8. 1. Woman, 25 years. L. 184, B. 150, C.I. 83·3, H. 122, Bz. 131, Orbit 28/36, Nose 21/41. Mouth projects forward, double curve.
8. Ofnet 18. 1. Woman, 30 years. L. 180, B. 142, C.I. 78·9, H. 120, Bz. 134, Orbit 29/32, Nose 23/42. Indications of double curve on left side.
9. Ofnet 25. 1. Woman, 20 years. L. 174, B. 136, C.I. 78·2, H. 127, Bz. 133, Orbit 26/35, Nose 30/47. Double curve, face broad, chin moderate, mouth projects forward.
10. Ofnet 2. 11. Woman, 20 years. L. 175, B. 136, C.I. 77·7, H. 128, Bz. 124, Orbit 29/30, Nose 23/42. Double curve, face broad, chin moderate.
11. Ofnet 5. 11. Woman, 22 years. L. 174, B. 134, C.I. 77·0, H. 125, Bz. 128, Orbit 30/40, Nose 22/40. Double curve, nose projects from a deep root, face broad, chin strong.
12. Ofnet 15. 1. Woman, 30 years. L. 177, B. 136, C.I. 76·8, H. 118, Bz. 123, Orbit 26/34, Nose 20/41. Brow ridges fairly marked, face broad, chin strong.
13. Ofnet 13. 1. Woman, 22 years. L. 177, B. 134, C.I. 75·7, H. 132, Bz. 121, Orbit 26/36, Nose 22/44. Face broad, chin fairly strong.
14. Ofnet 14. 1. Woman, 18 years. L. 187, B. 136, C.I. 72·7, H. 140, Bz. 113, Orbit 28/33, Nose 23/38. Mouth projects forward strongly, chin strong, face broad.
15. Ofnet. Several skulls of children.
16. Kaufertsberg (Lierheim, Nordlingen). L. 182, B. 141, C.I. 77·5, H. 139, Auric. H. 117. Brow ridges fairly strong, glabella strong. Bz. 125, Orbit 29/41, Nose 26/48. Face long, chin strong.
17. Furfooz, Belgium. 1. Young man. L. 174, B. 138, C.I. 79·3, H. 135, Bz. 135, Orbit 31/35, Nose 25/45, C.C. 1300. Brow ridges very moderate, forehead low, narrow, and receding.
18. Furfooz. 2. Woman ? L. 172, B. 140, C.I. 81·4, H. 134, Bz. 130, Orbit 30/39, Nose 24/49. Brow ridges weak, nose projecting.
19. Nagy Sap, Hungary. Man, 20–25 years. L. 170, B. 144, C.I. 84·7.
20. Mugem, Portugal. Man. L. 172, B. 142, C.I. 82·6, Bz. 146 ?, Orbit 33/37, prognathous.
21. Mugem. Probably a woman. Apparent C.I. 97·4, but probably posthumously deformed.

22. Mugem. Man. Brachycephalic, large brow ridges quite separate from one another.
23. Mugem. Woman. L. 173, B. 127, C.I. 73·4, H. 131, Bz. 121, Orbit 27/36, Nose 22/44. Orbits low and rectangular, mouth projects.
24. Val de Areeiro. Woman ? L. 171, B. 137, C.I. 80·1. Age doubtful.
25. Romanelli, Italy. L. 182, B. 144, C.I. 79·1, H. 149, Bz. 131, Orbit 32/37, Nose 23/50, C.C. 1575. Stature 1690, face long. This may be of any late palaeolithic period.
26. Olmo, Italy. L. 202, B. 150, C.I. 74·0, auricular height 116, capacity large. Age doubtful.
27. Staengenaes, Denmark. Woman. L. 200, B. 147, C.I. 73·5. Age doubtful.
28. Staengenaes. Sex ? L. 196, B. 147, C.I. 75. Age doubtful.
29. Svaerdborg, Denmark. Weak chin, molar teeth with five tubercles on each, 3rd molar the largest tooth, forearm has a curved radius ; all these are ancient features. The lower limb is more modern in type.

Note.—The period to which the Grenelle skulls belong is so uncertain that it has been thought best to omit them from this list. From Grenelle have been obtained skulls of both broad-headed and long-headed people. Details may be found in *Crania Ethnica*, by de Quatrefages and Hamy.

B. BRITISH SKULLS WHICH ARE KNOWN TO BE LATE PLEISTOCENE OR ARE OF DOUBTFUL AGE AND POSSIBLY LATE PLEISTOCENE.

1. Cheddar. Man. Stature 1620 (64″), L. 196, B. 138, C.I. 70·4, Bz. 139, Orbit 32/40. Head high, brow ridges moderate, face fairly broad, nose rather narrow, chin well marked.
2. Muskham, Trent Valley. Man. L. 180, B. 137, C.I. 76. Auricular height 122. Head high and ridged.
3. Ledbury. Man. L. 181, B. 139, C.I. 77·0. Strong brow ridges.
4. Tilbury. Man. L. 188, B. 142, C.I. 75·5. Auricular height 118. Head high and ridged. Date doubtful, may be more recent.
5. Halling. Man, under 40. L. 187, B. 142, C.I. 75·9. Auricular height 124, Bz. 140, Stature 1630. Head very high, brow ridges moderate, chin moderate.

6. Langwith. Man. L. 192, B. 135, C.I. 70·3, Auricular height 127, C.C. 1250. Head very high and ridged, brow ridges strong.
7. Dartford. Man. L. 207, B. 150, C.I. 73, Auricular height 129, C.C. 1750. Head high and ridged.
8. Cissbury. Man. L. 184, B. 132, C.I. 71·0, H. 140, C.C. 1350.
9. Cissbury. Woman. L. 195, B. 144, C.I. 74·0, C.C. 1732.

    Of the above, No. 1 is almost certainly of the end of the Palaeolithic Age. Nos. 2–7 may be of that age or later. Nos. 8 and 9 are of disputed age, some identifying them as palaeolithic, others as of the transition from palaeolithic to neolithic or even later.

10. Galley Hill. L. 204, B. 140, C.I. 68·6. Strong brow ridges, high head. C.C. 1350–1500. Stature 1600 (63″). Limbs modern in general features.

    Has been claimed to be early palaeolithic; many ascribe it to the end of the Palaeolithic Age.

11. Ipswich. L. 192, B. 144, C.I. 75·0, Auricular height 111, Bz. 135. Age very doubtful.
12. Baker's Hole. L. 195, B. 140, C.I. 72, Auricular height 118. Brow ridges well marked.
13. Aveline's Hole. Tardenoisian period.
  A. Sex doubtful, probably male, 40–60 years. L. 195, B. 138, C.I. 70·8, H. 136, Auricular height 117, C.C. 1440, Orbit 32/41, Bz. 140.
  B. Female, 40–50 years. L. 178, B. 143, C.I. 80·3.
  C. Male ?, 40 years. L. 178, B. 142, C.I. 80·0.
  D. Male, probably under 45 years. L. 188, B. 134, C.I. 71·3, C.C. 1426 (at Oxford).
14. Oban. Probably of Tardenoisian period.
  A. MacArthur Cave. Young male. L. 183, B. 138, C.I. 75·4, H. 139, Orbit 33/40, Nose 23/48.
  B. MacArthur Cave. Male. L. 205, B. 144, C.I. 70·2, H. ?, Orbit 31/42, Nose ?. A high skull with strong brow ridges.
  C. Mackay Cave. A child. L. 171, B. 133, C.I. 77·8.

BOOKS
(*See Chapter 5*)

9
Chronological Summary

IN the foregoing chapters we have been relating the story of the gradual passing away of the last glaciation, known as the Würm Ice Age. This is believed to have reached its greatest intensity about 23,000 B.C., though this date is based only on a very rough calculation. During its maximum extension the land was, we believe, elevated about 800 feet above its present level, the snow-fields and glaciers in the Alps and elsewhere in Central Europe reached down 1,200 metres below their present position, while an extensive ice-sheet, covering Scandinavia and Finland, stretched southwards of the southern shore of the Baltic, ending in what is known as the line of the Daniglacial moraines.

Gradually the severity of the climate lessened, the land sank, the snow-fields and glaciers retreated, and the northern ice-sheet shrank, leaving the deposits of the Daniglacial retreat. This is called the Laufen retreat, but it lasted only for a time. Then a return of the cold followed a re-elevation of the land, and we get the second maximum of the Würm, which can, with fair precision, be dated at 13,500 B.C. The Alpine glaciers again descended, and the northern ice-sheet advanced to the line of the Gothiglacial moraines. Then a further amelioration of the climate ensued, lasting for about 3,000 years. On the whole the ice retreated, though sometimes a slight re-advance occurred. This is the time known in the Alps as the Achen oscillation, and in the Baltic as the Gothiglacial retreat.

We have seen that, not long before the first maximum of the

Würm Ice Age, Neanderthal men with their Mousterian industry passed from the plain of north Germany into France and western Europe, which had been left free for them by the departure southwards of the people responsible for the Acheulian culture. As the intensity of the cold increased, some of these Neanderthal men, too, moved southwards, some going by Gibraltar to North Africa, while others, passing down Italy, endeavoured to cross by Sicily and Malta. Others remained behind, taking shelter in caves during the periods of extreme cold. These occupied various parts of Europe during the slightly milder conditions of the Laufen retreat, and survived the second maximum of the Würm, at any rate on the northern shores of the Mediterranean.

Meanwhile, another race of men, not unlike the present inhabitants of the world, and entitled to the specific name of *Homo sapiens*, appeared in North Africa. Whence they came is uncertain. It may have been from the Sahara, then enjoying an ample rainfall with plenty of grass, and perhaps forests as well, or they may have passed across the Sinaitic peninsula, then larger and less dry, from some part of south-west Asia. Their tools were finely made from relatively small flakes of flint, and, as their industry was first noticed at Gafsa, in Tunisia, the ancient Capsa, it has been termed Capsian. Archaeologists have recognized two types of this industry, an eastern or Getulian and a western or Ibero-Maurusian. Whether these two types developed contemporaneously in different areas in North Africa, or whether they indicate two successive waves of immigrants, is not yet clear, but both types ultimately reached Europe.

It must have been some time during the Würm glaciation that certain members of the Getulian branch crossed over the land bridge then existing between Tunisia and Sicily and spread up into Italy, but it was not, we believe, until well

Chronological Summary 137

after the passing of the second maximum that they reached the south of France. Here they arrived, we believe, about 11,000 B.C., introducing what is known as Aurignacian culture. Either here or on the way hither they seem to have come into

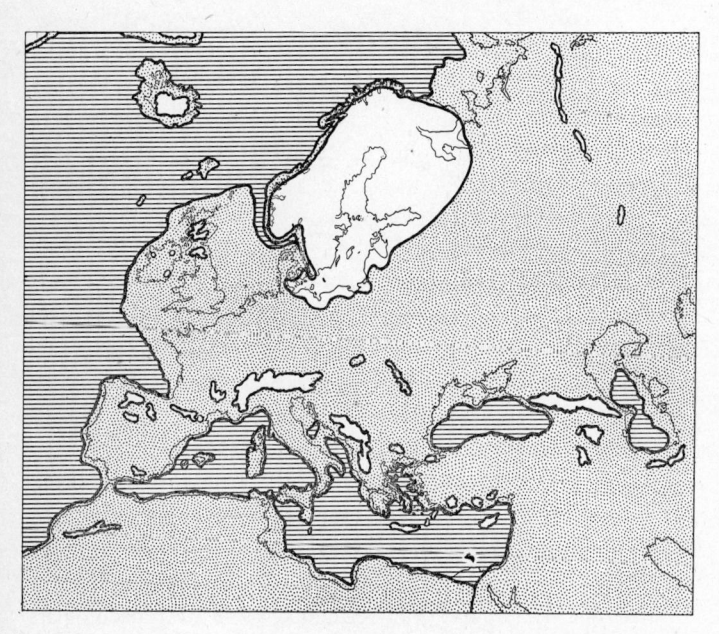

FIG. 74. Map of Europe during the second maximum of the Würm glaciation.

contact with the Mousterian culture of their Neanderthal predecessors, for at some of their earliest settlements in France, such as the rock-shelter at Audi, we find certain implements, known as Audi points, which show a close resemblance to some Mousterian tools.

As far as we can judge these new-comers were not all exactly of one type, for there are considerable differences to be observed among the skeletons from the earliest deposits. One type, the Grimaldi, is of moderate stature, with a long narrow head and a slightly protruding jaw. Only two skeletons of this type have as yet been found, and these date from the very beginning of the period; but types closely resembling these are not uncommonly met with among the present population of North Africa. Another well-known type, the Cro-Magnon, possessed very great stature, and a long, narrow, but low head with a short and broad face. The Predmost–Combe Capelle, with a long, narrow but high head, will soon be best known from Predmost specimens, and may represent a fresh set of intruders. Besides these three main types there are other individuals showing intermediate traits. The variation in stature and head form is considerable, though the heads of all were relatively long and narrow.

Three distinct phases of this Aurignacian culture can be distinguished in France, which have been termed Lower, Middle, and Upper, and these seem to have lasted from about 11,500 to 10,000 B.C. Throughout all this time these Aurignacian men continued to carve figures and engrave small objects, and to decorate the walls of the caves which they inhabited. These figures were more often those of women, generally of fat women, during the earlier part of the period, while engravings of animals, such as those they hunted for food, take their place towards the end.

Early in the Upper Aurignacian period the climate became still milder, and the vegetation in the north European plain gradually changed from the tundra conditions, which had obtained at first, to those of a cold grassy steppe. Herds of hoofed animals came in from the east, and it may be that it was in pursuit that Predmost–Combe Capelle men arrived in west Europe. Soon afterwards, rather before 10,000 B.C., a new industry appeared in the east, gradually spreading north-westwards, which was to effect a considerable change.

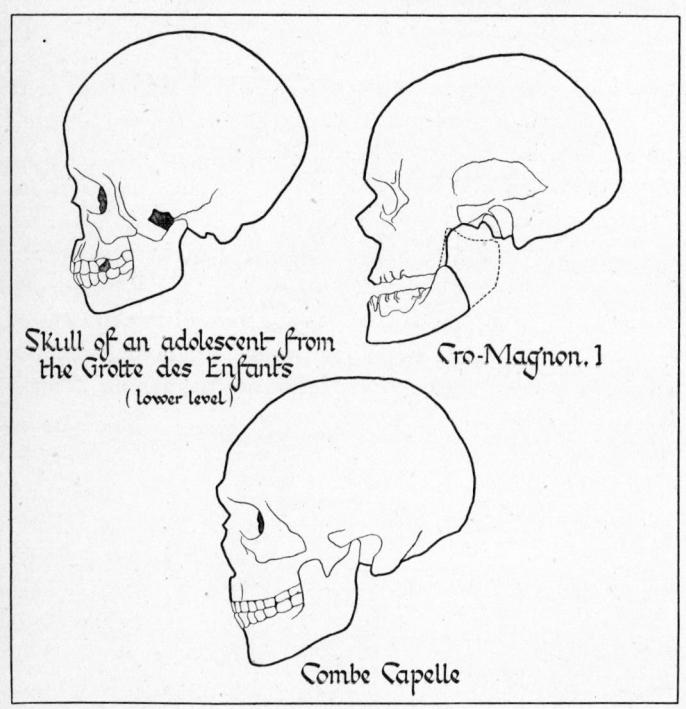

FIG. 75. Profiles of Grimaldi, Cro-Magnon, and Combe Capelle skulls.

We must now, however, retrace our steps to follow the adventures of the western group of Capsians, the Ibero-Maurusians. About 11,000 B.C. some of these seem to have crossed the Straits of Gibraltar into Spain and by degrees to have occupied the eastern part of that peninsula. They carried with them a culture in many ways resembling that which they had in North Africa. Only one feature has not yet been noticed on the southern side of the straits, and that is their art. These people, with what is known as Early Capsian culture, made little pictures on the surface of the stone beneath overhanging rocks, and in these they portrayed scenes of life in a very vivid manner. This art is well developed in the earliest stages which we meet with in Spain, and we feel convinced that still earlier phases of it will some day be discovered in Morocco. The first phase of this industry, the Early Capsian, with the earlier stages of its 'East Spanish' art, lasted on until about 9500 B.C., when it developed into the type known as Late Capsian.

We must now return to the new invaders of north Europe, who came from the east in the wake of the hoofed animals of the steppe. Their culture, called Solutrean after Solutré near Macon in Burgundy, appeared first in Hungary, in an early form known as Proto-Solutrean, and thence spread across north Germany to Belgium and the north of France. This new industry is characterized by its highly finished spearheads, shaped like laurel or willow leaves, worked all over with very fine pressure-flaking. This proto-Solutrean industry appeared in the plain while the Upper Aurignacian still held possession of the mountains, but eventually, with the arrival of the true Solutrean period, about 10,000 B.C., when the laurel leaf blades attained their finest form, the invaders made themselves masters of all the country north of the Pyrenees. Of what type these invaders were is uncertain, but as a number of skeletons resembling that from Combe Capelle have been found in Moravia, apparently dating from this time, we may suspect that the invaders were of that type. That they came from the east seems certain, for implements of the earliest proto-Solutrean type have been found in Hungary, and we

Chronological Summary

can have little doubt that the advent of steppe conditions during the closing phase of the Aurignacian period brought not only the steppe fauna with its hoofed animals, but in due course the men accustomed to hunt them. That they were an active, vigorous people, accustomed to hunting on foot the

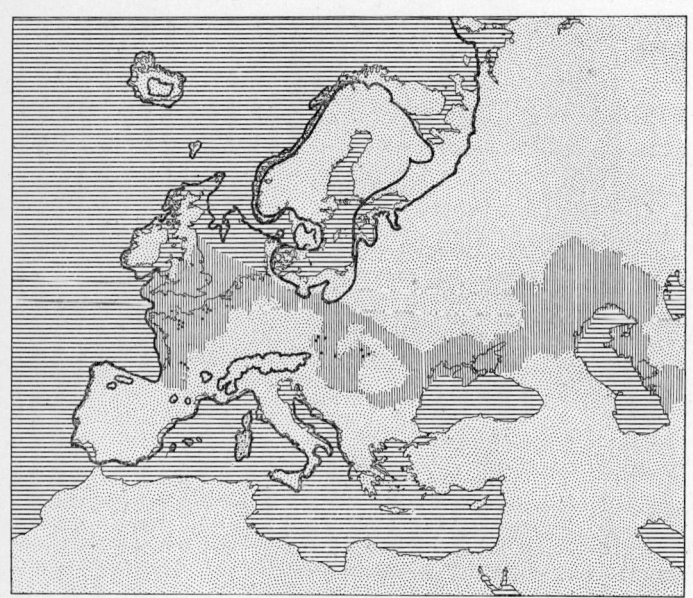

FIG. 76. Map showing the distribution of the Proto-Solutrean industry.

fleet inhabitants of the steppe, seems certain; they had brought their weapons of the chase to a high pitch of perfection, and, in so far as we can judge, they were not given to those artistic efforts for which the Aurignacians were so justly famous.

Not long after 10,000 B.C. another slight elevation is known to have begun in the Baltic region; this extended, in all probability, throughout Europe, and accounted for a slight lowering of the temperature. This movement we are equating with the first instance of the triple advance of the glaciers, still known, for convenience, as the Bühl. At the same time the storm zone, which had traversed the Sahara during the Würm maximum, and had been moving north in the interval, had reached the Mediterranean, and conditions in north Europe were not so dry as they had been. The grassy steppes began to give way gradually to pine forests, which spread north-westwards over Europe from the Caucasus; the hoofed animals for the most part retreated to Asia, whence they had come, and many of the Solutrean hunters followed them. Those who were left, mixed doubtless with such Aurignacians as had remained, lingered on in southern France, with an industry known as Upper Solutrean. Meanwhile, those of the Aurignacians who had fled to northern Spain, and had been living in the caves there beyond the reach of the Solutreans, had been developing a new culture. Since flint was scarce in their new abodes they depended less upon this as a raw material than upon bone, out of which they fashioned many new types of implements; such as they continued to make of flint were very much smaller and fewer in number. As the first Bühl phase came to an end about 9500 B. C., the Upper Solutrean remnant seems to have diminished in number and importance, and the people from the north Spanish caves returned to their old haunts, introducing the culture known as Magdalenian from the cave of La Madeleine in the Dordogne, where it was first discovered.

The Magdalenian period, as it is called, lasted from about 9500 to 6500 B. C. During the whole time the climate was somewhat inclement and wet, but during some centuries more so than during others. We have seen that the land around the Baltic was somewhat elevated soon after 10,000 B. C., and we have presumed that the same was true elsewhere in Europe.

Chronological Summary 143

Further similar elevations took place about 8500 B.C., and again about 6500 B.C. These three elevations, with their corresponding periods of cold, we have equated with the triple expansion of the Alpine glaciers, still known as Bühl. During the second of these were laid down the Fenno-Scandian

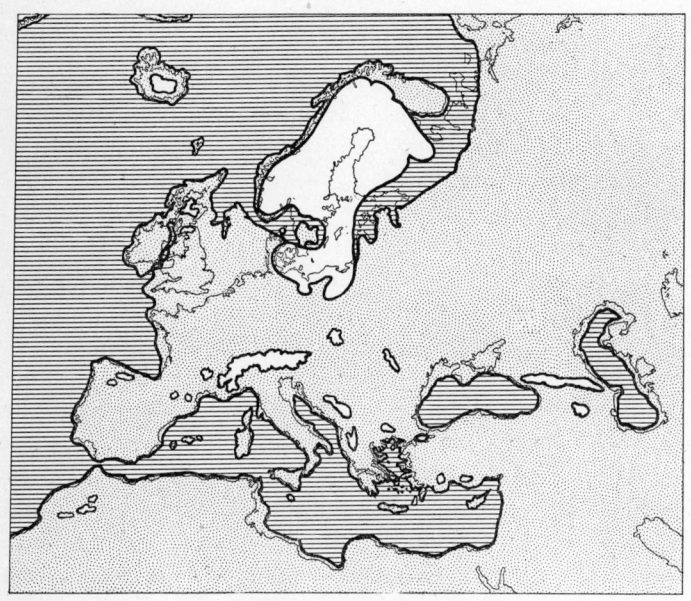

FIG. 77. Europe in 2nd Würm maximum.
Note:—For Bühl glaciation see Fig. 3, Edge of Finiglacial ice sheet.

moraines, which stretch across the Swedish lakes, and during the third took place what is known as the Ragunda pause. During all three, we believe, were formed those moraines which are to be seen by the sides of several of the Swiss lakes.

The Lower Magdalenian phases, numbered 1, 2, and 3, lasted from about 9500 to 8000 B.C., and during the latter part of this occurred the second Bühl phase, when Arctic rodents took refuge in the caves of Switzerland. About this time the Baltic Sea was almost wholly free from ice, and a great sheet of water, known as the Yoldia Sea, connected the Arctic Ocean near what is now the Murmansk coast with the southern part of the North Sea. This Yoldia Sea lasted from before 8000 to after 7000 B.C.

The Middle Magdalenian phases, numbered 4 and 5, lasted from 8000 to 7000 B.C., while the remaining 500 years was occupied by the Late Magdalenian phase, No. 6, which came to an end about 6500 B.C., at the time of the third cold period of the Bühl. Meanwhile, what is known as the Late Capsian industry, with its later phases of east Spanish art, was flourishing in eastern Spain. There is no need here to recapitulate the distinctions between the different phases of the industries nor to trace the evolution of the round harpoons of reindeer horn, for these have been described in a former chapter. Nor, for the same reason, is it necessary to repeat the descriptions of the several phases of the art, which rose at first to the finest style of cave art, then grew careless, degenerated, and finally collapsed with great suddenness at the close of the period. Nor need we describe again the type of man who was living here at that time. No skeletons have been found that differ profoundly enough from those discovered in Aurignacian deposits to lead us to suspect the arrival of a new people.

About 7000 B.C. the storm zone, which had for many centuries traversed the Mediterranean, began to shift farther north, and the heaviest precipitation fell north of the Alpine-Pyrenean line. With this mildness and moisture the pines began to give way to oaks, and dense forests with tangled undergrowth spread to all regions, but those in which the subsoil was light and porous, as was the case in some limestone hills, chalk downs, and sandy loess deposits. The open lands, filled with game, were much restricted, and the Magdalenian folk, who had hunted this game, found their food supplies diminishing.

There was, too, another effect of the shifting of the storm zone. As long as this had traversed the Mediterranean, the Sahara, Arabia and Persia had experienced a light but regular rainfall, more intense in the west but not negligible in the east. These regions, which had perhaps been partly wooded during the Würm glaciation, had been grassy steppe-lands for very many centuries, and the game which abounds on such steppes had doubtless sustained a fairly large population. The gradual northward shifting of the storm zone by degrees reduced this rainfall, until eventually these regions became the deserts which we know to-day.

The diminution of the rainfall, and of the grass and of the hoofed animals which lived on it, must have sadly reduced the food supply, and so we might expect a great exodus. That this happened we may gather from the sudden appearance of a new industry in Spain, whence it passed to north and east Europe, in the Nile valley, the Jordan valley, Mesopotamia, eastern India and Ceylon. This industry, which consisted of very small geometric flint implements, is known generically as microlithic, in North Africa and Spain as Final Capsian, and in France and elsewhere in Europe as Tardenoisian. Soon after 7000 B.C. the people responsible for this industry seem to have spread in all directions and, though the subsidence of the land bridge prevented them from passing to Sicily, they succeeded in crossing the Straits of Gibraltar, if not altogether dryshod.

Of what type were these Final Capsian invaders it is not easy to decide, but it seems likely that they were long-heads, as were their predecessors, and that, indeed, they carried on the Aurignacian-Solutrean-Magdalenian types, especially those with high-ridged, narrow heads. Thus may have reached the shores of the western Mediterranean and the seaboard of south-west Europe and the British Isles the effective basis of the small, slight, long-headed brunette people, including persons with characters obviously derived from such types as Grimaldi and Predmost–Combe Capelle, who still live there. These elements, indeed, form the basis of the population of south-west Europe, and are known as the Mediterranean Race. We thus deem that race to have arisen by the intermingling of Aurignacian, Solutrean, Magdalenian, and Final Capsian elements, mostly fairly akin, in south-west Europe, and to have undergone modification in certain directions, notably by the reduction of some ancient inheritances in the course of its history there. The rarity of strains clearly derived from the Cro-Magnon stock in the Mediterranean Race of subsequent periods is a remarkable fact, though Collignon found traces of it in the Dordogne, and it is said to occur in the Pyrenees and among the Tuareg of the Sahara.

As we have seen, the advance-guard of the invaders amalgamated with a remnant of the Magdalenian folk in Cantabria, and jointly they developed the Lower Azilian culture. Later, before 6000 B.C., another wave entered France to the east of the Pyrenees and proceeded across that country, introducing there the Tardenoisian culture. Some of these picked up elements of Lower Azilian culture and combined it with their own. Thus an Azilian-Tardenoisian culture spread over the greater part of Europe, more Azilian in the west and by the sea, but more Tardenoisian eastwards and inland. The migrants probably combined with survivors of the Predmost group on the loess of central and eastern Europe, and it is further probable that these various elements contributed in due course to the evolution of the Nordic Race Type.

Meanwhile, a new people had been approaching Europe

from the east. We do not know what elements of culture they brought with them, for in the earliest deposit we have, at Ofnet in Bavaria, their industry had both Tardenoisian and Azilian elements, picked up apparently after their arrival.

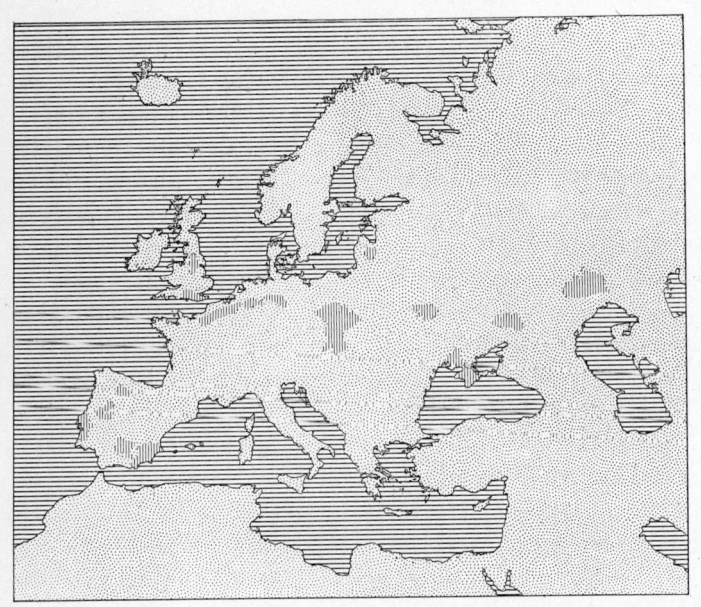

FIG. 78. Map showing the distribution of the Tardenoisian industry in Europe.

These people were broad-headed, that is to say the breadth of their heads was more than 80 per cent. of the length. The supposition is that, like subsequent invasions of broad-headed people, they came from Asia, the home of broad-heads. They seem to have arrived in central Europe by 6000 B.C., and must have spread gradually among the Azilian-Tardenoisian folk, adopting their culture, for skulls of their type have been found at Furfooz in Belgium and at Grenelle near Paris. Not much later we find some broad skulls among the population at Mugem on the Tagus, not far from Lisbon, where there was a riverside settlement, with a Final Capsian culture, but dating, it would seem, from between 6000 and 5000 B. C.

During the whole of this time, from 6500 to 5500 B. C., the various peoples were leading a hard existence, those with the more Azilian type of culture living sometimes in caves, but more often by the banks of lakes and rivers, or by the sea-shore, feeding on shell-fish, nuts, and berries, fish and a little flesh food. Those with the more Tardenoisian culture, with the exception of those at Mugem, seem to have hunted in their restricted grounds on the open sandy loess or on the limestone plateaux.

We have seen that there was a slight elevation of the land and a recurrence of cold about 6500 B. C.; this caused the Baltic Sea, which had during the Yoldia period been open to the Arctic Ocean and the North Sea, to become closed at both ends, thus forming the Ancylus Lake or inland sea. What is now Denmark thus arose above the water for the first time since the ice-sheet had left it, and we find there a culture, called the Nörre-Lyngby culture, which contains elements not introduced by the spread of the Tardenoisians, who had scarcely yet reached such northern latitudes.

It will be remembered that on the arrival of the Solutrean invaders many of the Aurignacians fled to the Pyrenees, where they developed the distinctive traits of Magdalenian culture. Elsewhere, too, they took to the mountains, but when the danger was passed, these refugees, like the Magdalenians, descended to the plains, with a developed Aurignacian culture. They must have had some intercourse with their Magdalenian neighbours, as objects of true Magdalenian workmanship have been found in the Mendips, Derbyshire and elsewhere, but on the whole the cultures of these more northern and eastern peoples developed on their own lines. We may conjecture that they moved northwards as the Tardenoisians

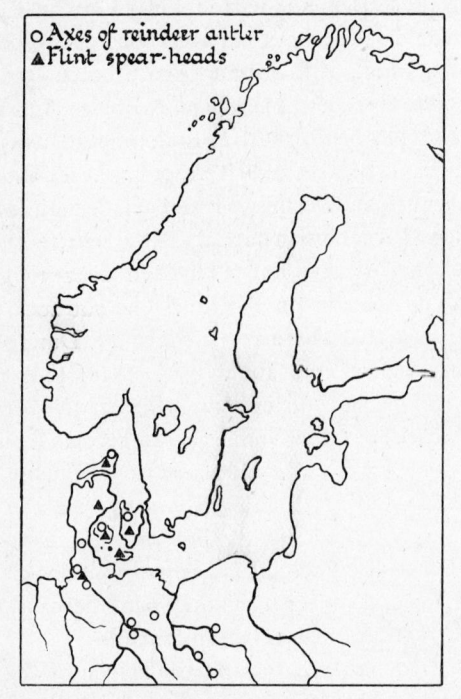

FIG. 79. Map showing the distribution of the Nörre-Lyngby culture.

advanced, and that the Nörre-Lyngby culture, and others to be mentioned later, were developed from these Aurignacian survivals, mingled perhaps with some other elements. The Nörre-Lyngby culture began soon after 6000 B.C., and lasted to 5500 B.C. or later, and was succeeded by the Maglemose, which extended from Denmark to East Prussia, and westwards to Holderness. This, which included some implements of definitely Tardenoisian type, lasted until after 5000 B.C., when it was succeeded by the Svaerdborg culture, much more Tardenoisian in type, which in turn continued until nearly 4000 B.C.

About 4500 B.C. there was another slight rise in the land and lowering of the temperature, which we may equate with the Gschnitz stage in the Alps. After this the land sank to about twenty-five feet below its present level, and the climate grew milder than it is now. The North Sea broke through the islands of Denmark, thus converting the Baltic into a very salt sea, the Littorina Sea.

The Scandinavian geologists believe that the Littorina period lasted from before 4000 B.C. to about 200 B.C., when the coast-line reached its present level. During the first thousand years of this period the people of the Baltic were living by the sea-shore, feeding on fish, shell-fish and occasional small animals. Elsewhere much the same kind of life was being followed by the waterside, and on the dry, open lands the people lived more on berries, nuts, or roots. To dig up the latter, it has been suggested, they developed a kind of pick or hoe, known sometimes as the Thames pick or the Campignian pick, and the whole period, from about 4000 to 3000 B.C. or even later, is sometimes called the Campignian period.

Thus from a free and open hunting life the people of north-western Europe had been reduced to the status of the poorest food-collectors, in spite of two infusions of fresh population from the steppes of Asia and Africa. The closing in of the oak forest, completing the destruction of their hunting-grounds, was the main cause of this degeneration, and it seems likely that our predecessors would have remained for ever in this backward state, had not movements from the east brought a fresh impetus into their lives.

INDEX

Abri Mège, 81.
Achen stage, 4, 5, 11, 22, 23, 30–40, 91, 135.
Acheulian culture, 42, 48, 136.
Adriatic Sea, 22.
Aegean Sea, 22.
Africa, North, 12, 20, 22, 39, 46, 48, 59, 64, 73, 88, 96, 97, 136, 138, 140, 145, 150.
Africa, South, 88.
Albacete, 93.
Alcadi de Rio, 84.
Alcolea, 76.
Allier, 46.
Alpera, 93.
Alps, 1, 2, 5, 10, 12, 23, 28, 32, 38, 39, 41, 50, 55, 91, 107, 108, 125, 126, 135, 143, 144, 150.
America, North, 8, 32.
Anatolia, 125.
Ancylus Lake, 21, 24, 25, 28, 96, 108, 148.
Ancylus period, 26, 27, 36, 99, 102, 105–8.
Arabia, 97, 145.
Arctic Ocean, 23, 30, 95, 144, 148.
Arctic regions, 34.
Ardeche, 50.
Ariège, 82.
Armstrong, A. Leslie, 106, 114.
Asia, 32, 49, 136, 142, 147, 150.
Asiatic steppe, 104.
Asturian culture, 107, 119, 120.
Asturias, 118.
Atlantic region, 34.
Audi rock-shelter, 41, 44, 46, 137.
Audi points, 43, 46, 137.
Aurignac, 40, 131.
Aurignacian culture, 40–2, 44–8, 50, 53, 56–9, 81, 84, 90, 91, 137–40, 144, 146, 148.
Aurignacian men, 46, 52, 58, 59, 62, 66, 86, 88, 92, 122, 129, 138, 141, 142, 148.
Aurignacian period, 44, 46, 48, 50, 62, 67, 69, 79, 80, 82–4, 86, 116, 121, 138, 141.
Austria, 48, 58.
Aveline's Hole, 121, 128, 130, 134.
Azilian culture, 98–100, 102–4, 107, 108, 146–8.

Baker's Hole, 134.
Ballahöhle, 74.
Baltic region, 2, 5–8, 22, 28, 36, 105, 110, 141.
Baltic Sea, 6, 14, 23, 24, 38, 95, 102, 106, 108, 135, 142, 144, 148, 150.
Baltic States, 23.
Bann River, 105, 114, 118.
Barma Grande, 80.
Basle, 102.
Bavaria, 38, 50, 100, 123, 147.
Bégouen, Count, 82, 83.
Belgium, 48, 50, 58, 106, 132, 140, 148.
Birkner, F., 123.
Black Sea, 29.
Blangy-sur-Bresle, 112.
Bohemia, 31, 48, 104.

Bonn, 75.
Boswell, P. G. H., 10.
Boule, M., 77.
Bouyssonie, l'Abbé J., 47.
Braband culture, 108, 110.
Breuil, l'Abbé H., 35, 36, 41, 42, 47, 53, 57, 81, 84–7, 90, 97, 103, 105, 106.
British Isles, 2, 14, 15, 26, 50, 58, 100, 128, 131, 146.
Brøgger, W. C., 10, 115.
Brooks, C. E. P., 12.
Brückner, E., 4, 5.
Bruges, 93.
Brünn Race, 67, 73, 74, 92, 121, 127.
Bühl advance, 4, 5, 10–12, 22, 23, 25, 30, 36, 37, 55, 91, 95, 96, 107, 142–4.
Bulgaria, 48.
Burgundy, 140.
Burkitt, M., 58, 95.
Bushmen, 88.

Campignian culture, 107, 114, 116, 150.
Campigny, Le, 112, 117.
Cantabria, 36, 98, 102, 146.
Capitan, L., 86, 105.
Capsa, 40, 136.
Capsian culture, 40, 41, 44, 90, 91, 96, 102, 107, 136, 140, 144–6, 148.
Capsian men, 88, 92, 94, 96, 102, 106, 116, 139.
Carpathians, 104.
Caspian Sea, 29.
Castellón, 90.
Casterley Camp, 114.
Castillo, 84, 87.
Cattegat, 23.
Caucasus, 142.
Ceylon, 96, 98, 145.
Chancelade, 75.
Châtelperron, 42, 44, 46.
Cheddar, 127, 133.
Chellean culture, 42.
Childe, V. Gordon, 120.
Christy, H., 53, 65.
Chwalibogowice, 105, 118.
Cissbury, 117, 134.
Collignon, R., 67, 146.
Combarelles, 35, 85.
Combe Capelle type, 66–71, 92, 121, 127–9, 138–40, 146.
Cooke, J. H., 27.
Cordoba, 76.
Corsica, 22.
Cracow, 105.
Creswell Crags, 57.
Crimea, 104.
Cro-Magnon Race, 59, 65–8, 70, 71, 92, 127, 138, 139, 146.
Cueva del Civil, 90.
Cueva del Mas d'en Josep, 89.
Cunnington, Mrs., 114.
Czecho-Slovakia, 70.

Index

Daniglacial moraine, 6, 8, 10, 11, 135.
Daniglacial retreat, 6, 7, 10, 135.
Dartford, 134.
Daun stage, 5, 11, 25, 37.
Debenham, F., 3.
Denmark, 14, 23, 28, 37, 96, 105, 106, 108, 111, 112, 120, 133, 149.
Depéret, C., 13.
Derbyshire, 57, 148.
Dogger Bank, 27.
Dordogne, 41, 46, 50, 52, 53, 71, 142, 146.
Durham, 100.

East Spanish art, 64, 87, 92, 140, 144.
Egypt, 96.
Elasmothere, 32, 33.
England, 10, 14, 27, 39, 48, 104, 110, 112, 114.
Enquist, F., 7.
Enzheim, 73.
Epipalaeolithic Age, 107, 120.
Ertebölle, 107, 109, 112.
Estonia, 108, 109, 112.
Euphrates valley, 98.
Europe, 1, 12, 14, 19, 23, 30–2, 34–8, 40, 48, 49, 54, 59, 60, 62, 69, 77–9, 91, 95–8, 104, 110, 114, 116, 118, 127, 129, 131, 136, 137, 139, 140, 141, 143, 145–8, 150.
Europe, Central, 1, 5, 31, 36, 48, 50, 70, 80, 81, 135.

Fennoscandian moraine, 8, 10, 11, 23, 25, 37, 143.
Fère-en-Tardenois, 103.
Finiglacial retreat, 7, 8, 10, 25, 28, 37.
Finland, 2, 8, 9, 23, 135.
Florence, 93.
Font-de-Gaume, 86.
Forestian periods, 11, 25.
France, 27, 35, 39, 46, 48, 50, 52, 56–8, 76, 81, 88, 91, 92, 94, 100, 102, 106, 116, 120, 136, 137, 140, 144–6.
Funen, 6.
Furfooz, 125, 132, 148.
Fürst, C. M., 70.

Gafsa, 40, 136.
Galley Hill, 129, 134.
Geer, Baron de, 5, 7, 8, 10.
Geikie, James, 10, 12.
Germany, 48, 58, 75, 104, 136.
Germany, North, 2, 140.
Getulian culture, 40, 140.
Ghar Dalam, 14, 16, 17.
Gibraltar, 136.
Gibraltar, Straits of, 14, 21, 22, 88, 139, 145.
Gironde, 44.
Giuffrida-Ruggeri, V., 70.
Gothiglacial moraine, 6, 8, 10, 11, 25, 37, 135.
Gothiglacial retreat, 6–8, 10, 23, 25, 30, 37, 135.
Greenland, 1.
Grenelle, 148.
Grimaldi Race, 63, 64, 66, 70–2, 92, 138, 139, 146.
Grimes Graves, 114, 116, 117.

Grotte des Enfants, 94.
Gschnitz stage, 5, 11, 12, 23, 25, 27, 37, 38, 107, 108, 150.
Guernsey, 39.
Günz glaciation, 12.

Halling, 128, 133.
Hamster, 33.
Hanover, 106.
Harz mountains, 31.
Hauser, O., 69.
Haute-Garonne, 40.
Holderness, 106–8, 150.
Homo sapiens, 1, 136.
Hungary, 31, 50, 81, 132, 140.
Hussowitz, 74.

Iberian peninsula, 27, 40.
Ibero-Marusian culture, 40, 136, 139.
Ice Age, 1, 8, 12, 26, 38.
India, 96, 98, 145.
Ipswich, 134.
Ireland, 38, 105, 106, 114, 120.
Irkutsk, 106.
Islandmagee, 120.
Italy, 20, 22, 40, 46, 48, 133, 136.

Jerboa, great, 33.
Jersey, 18, 39.
Jordan valley, 98, 145.
Jutland, 6, 14, 108, 109.

Kaufertsberg, 132.
Keith, Sir Arthur, 27, 61, 77.
Kennet valley, 110.
Kiang, 33.
Kirghiz Steppe, 104.
Kirkcudbright, 100.
Klaatsch, H., 66, 70.
Klause, 74.
Königsberg, 23.
Kozłowski, L., 105, 106, 114.
Krapina, 18.
Kunda, 108–10.

La Faye Bruniquel, 75.
La Ferrassie, 46.
La Gravette point, 46, 48.
La Madeleine, 53, 142.
Lamothe, L., 13.
Lancashire, 14.
Langwith, 128, 134.
Larne, 114.
Lartet, E., 53, 65.
Laufen retreat, 4, 11, 135, 136.
Laugerie Basse, 75, 95.
Laugerie Haute, 95.
Lautsch, 74.
Lea valley, 10.
Ledbury, 133.
Leghorn, 22.
Le Placard, 75.
Les Eyzies, 41.
Les Minquiers, 39.
Les Trois Frères, 85.
Lidén, R., 8.

Index

Lierheim, 132.
Lisbon, 102, 148.
Littorina Sea, 23–25, 27, 28, 38, 108, 112, 114, 150.
Lofotens, 7.
Loire, 50.
Lusitanian flora, 38.

Macalister, R. A. S., 58, 95, 120.
MacArthur Cave, 128, 134.
MacCurdy, G. G., 58, 95.
Mackay Cave, 134.
Macon, 48, 140.
Magdalenian culture, 52–8, 78, 79–85, 90, 91, 94–8, 100, 104–7, 116, 121, 129, 142–6, 148.
Maglemose culture, 106–10, 116, 149.
Majorca, 22.
Malta, 14, 18, 20, 136.
Marett, R. R., 18.
Mas d'Azil, 81, 98, 100–2.
Masurian Lakes, 30.
Mechta-el-Arbi, 73.
Mecklenburgian glaciation, 10–12, 25.
Mediterranean basin, 14, 18, 48, 54, 64, 97.
Mediterranean Sea, 13, 22, 39, 40, 95, 136, 142, 144–6.
Megaceros, 34.
Mendip caves, 57, 148.
Mentone, 36, 39.
Mesolithic Age, 82, 107, 120.
Mesopotamia, 12, 96, 145.
Mindel glaciation, 12.
Minorca, 22.
Miskolcz, 74.
Monaco, 53.
Montesquieu, 82.
Moravia, 50, 81, 140.
Morocco, 40.
Mortillet, G. de, 79.
Mousterian culture, 39, 42, 44, 46, 59, 78, 122, 136, 137.
Mugem, 102, 103, 107, 121, 126, 128, 132, 133, 140.
Mullerup, 106.
Murmansk coast, 144.
Muskham, 133.

Nagy Sap, 132.
Neanderthal man, 18, 19, 39, 59–61, 136, 137.
Neolithic Age, 27, 116.
Neu Essing, 74.
Newbury, 110.
New Caledonia, 122, 124.
Nigeria, 98.
Nile valley, 22, 98, 145.
Norde Fjord, 7.
Nordic Race, 146.
Nordlingen, 132.
Norfolk, 116.
Nörre-Lyngby culture, 105, 106, 114, 118, 148, 149.
Nøstvet, 112, 115.
North Sea, 14, 23, 27, 95, 108, 144, 148, 150.
Norway, 6, 10, 23, 112.

Oban, 100, 134.
Obercassel, 75.
Obermaier, H., 58, 77, 88, 90, 95, 100, 108, 109, 120, 122.
Ofnet, 38, 100, 121–3, 125–7, 131, 147.
Olmo, 133.
Oronsay, 100.
Osborn, H. Fairfield, 33.
Oundory, 77.

Pair-non-pair, 44.
Palaeolithic Age, 70, 77, 79, 82, 88, 91, 94, 95, 97, 106, 119, 121, 128, 129.
Palmer, L. S., 27.
Paris, 148.
Paviland Cave, 73.
Penck, A., 4, 5.
Persia, 97, 145.
Peyrony, D., 86, 105.
Piette, É., 78, 81.
Pleistocene period, 1, 12, 13, 14, 21.
Pocala, 39.
Poland, 48, 50, 58, 74, 104–6, 114.
Polonian glaciation, 10, 12.
Ponder's End, 10.
Portugal, 34, 127, 132.
Postglacial retreat, 7, 11, 25, 37.
Pre-Chellean culture, 42.
Predmost type, 67, 68, 74, 121, 127–9, 138, 146.
Prussia, 105.
Prussia, East, 30, 106, 149.
Prussia, West, 6.
Pyrenees, 36, 58, 92, 102, 140, 144, 146, 148.

Ra moraine, 6, 10.
Ragunda, Lake, 8.
Ragunda pause, 8, 11, 12, 23, 25, 37, 143.
Reid, Clement, 27.
Reinach, S., 80.
Reinecke, P., 109.
Rhone valley, 50.
Riga, Bay of, 6.
Riss glaciation, 12, 39.
Riviera, the, 41, 129.
Romanelli, 133.
Romsdal, 7.
Rostock, 6.
Roumania, 48.
Rügen, 105.
Russia, 23, 28–30, 48, 77, 104, 114.

Sahara Desert, 97, 98, 136, 145, 146.
Saiga, 36.
S. Girons, 82.
Samara, 77.
San Giorgio a Mare, 14.
Saône valley, 48, 50.
Sarasin, F., 122, 124.
Sardinia, 22.
Saxonian glaciation, 10, 12.
Scandinavia, 2, 5, 8, 23, 36, 110, 114, 135, 150.
Scania, 25, 105.
Scanian glaciation, 10, 12.

Index

Schmidt, R. R., 125.
Scotland, 10, 12–14, 24, 99, 104, 108.
Sederholme, J. J., 9.
Seine Inférieure, 112.
Settle, 100.
Shropshire, 30.
Siberia, 1, 32, 106.
Sicily, 14, 20, 40, 48, 136, 145.
Sierra, 84.
Sinaitic peninsula, 136.
Sollas, W. J., 8, 10, 12, 27, 58, 95, 120.
Solutré, 35, 36, 48, 67, 68, 73, 76, 121, 125, 129, 140.
Solutrean culture, 48–53, 56–8, 66, 81, 83, 84, 90, 91, 116, 121, 129, 140–2, 146, 148.
Solutrean period, 54.
Sorde, 75.
Spain, 22, 36, 38–40, 48, 50, 57, 76, 86, 88, 91, 92, 94, 96, 98, 100, 116, 118, 127, 139, 140, 142, 144, 145.
Stefansson, V., 34.
Stockholm, 6.
Strasbourg, 73.
Sudan, 64.
Sussex, 27.
Svaerdborg, 106, 107, 110, 133, 150.
Sweden, 6, 8, 23.
Swedish Lakes, 10, 143.
Swiss Lakes, 5, 143.
Switzerland, 55, 58, 102, 144.
Syria, 48, 96, 114.

Tagus, 102, 148.
Tardenoisian culture, 96, 103–7, 116, 121, 145–50.
Thames pick, 150.
Thatcham, 107, 110, 113.
Tierra del Fuego, 120.
Tilbury, 128, 133.
Trent valley, 133.
Trieste, 39.
Tuareg, 146.
Tuc d'Audoubert, 82, 83.
Tunis, 14, 21, 40.
Tunisia, 40, 44, 136.
Turbarian glaciations, 10–12, 25.
Turkestan, 49.

Ukraine, 29.

Val de Areeiro, 133.
Venice, 93.
Verneau, R., 63.
Villeneuve, l'Abbé, 64.
Viste, 108.
Vistula, 6, 105.
Volga, 77.

Wales, 104.
Warsaw, 6.
Wercholensk, 106.
Wener, Lake, 6.
Wetter, Lake, 6.
Whitburn, 100.
White Sea, 23.
Wied-x-Dalam, 14.
Wiltshire, 114.
Würm glaciation, 1, 4, 11, 12, 14, 18, 19, 22, 25, 30, 37, 39, 40, 55, 59, 79, 135–7, 142, 145.

Yenesei valley, 58.
Yoldia Sea, 20, 23–5, 28, 144, 148.
Yorkshire, 14, 100, 104, 106, 108.

Zealand, 6.